מסורה

The ArtScroll Series®

Rabbi Nosson Scherman / Rabbi Meir Zlotowitz
General Editors

KASHRUTH

A comprehensive background and reference guide to the principles of Kashruth

by Rabbi Yacov Lipschutz

Published by
Mesorah Publications, ltd

FIRST EDITION
First Impression . . . May, 1988

Published and Distributed by
MESORAH PUBLICATIONS, Ltd.
Brooklyn, New York 11223

Distributed in Israel by
MESORAH MAFITZIM / J. GROSSMAN
Rechov Harav Uziel 117
Jerusalem, Israel

Distributed in Europe by
J. LEHMANN HEBREW BOOKSELLERS
20 Cambridge Terrace
Gateshead, Tyne and Wear
England NE8 1RP

THE ARTSCROLL SERIES®
KASHRUTH

1969 Coney Island Avenue / Brooklyn, N.Y. 11223 / (718) 339-1700

ISBN:
0-89906-558-9 (hard cover)
0-89906-559-7 (paperback)

Printed in the United States of America by Noble Book Press Corp.
Bound by Sefercraft Quality Bookbinders, Ltd., Brooklyn, N.Y.

לזכר נשמות הני צנתרי דדהבה

הגאונים האדירים

מוה״ר לוי יוסף בן מו״ה שלמה זלמן ברייער זצ״ל

מוה״ר שלמה בן מו״ה שרגא הכהן רוזנברג זצ״ל

AN APPROBATION – מכתב ברכה

מרדכי גיפטער
ישיבת טלז
RABBI MORDECAI GIFTER
28570 NUTWOOD LANE
WICKLIFFE, OHIO 44092

ב"ה
כ"ב, בעומר. תשמ"ח

April 24, 1988

I am very impressed with the book on Kashrus by Rabbi Yacov Lipschutz of Monsey, N.Y.

He is a talmid chacham and a leading expert in the enormously complex field of kosher food production. To this field, Rabbi Lipschutz brings the rare but essential combination of authoritative halachic knowledge and expertise in the modern technology of food processing. In this book he shares this knowledge with the public, with the goal that every Jew should understand the basic principles of kashrus.

He is to be commended both for his clarity and his brevity. He has covered all angles of the subject without unnecessarily burdening the reader. He has seen to it that the reader will not reach halachic conclusions on his own. He has been careful to point out where rabbinic advice must be sought.

This book is a wonderful addition to the ArtScroll treasure house.

Mordekhai Gifter

AN APPROBATION – מכתב ברכה

בס״ד

ישיבה דפילאדעלפיא

הרב אלי׳ שוויי
ראש הישיבה

למע״כ ידידי ומחותני. הרה״ג הגאון ר׳ יצחק ד׳ הלוי ליבוביץ שליט״א

מגלגלין זכות על ידי זכאי. אחר שזכית לעמוד

על המערכה בעד קדושת ישראל ואלו עבדת עמדיך

אף על כל שאלו עליך כפי המסורת שקבלת מאבותיך ומגדולי

ישראל שעמדו הגאון על המערכה ועל כולם ועוצם לחמו

בעד מסורת ישראל בהתמדת הכוונות אלו ללחם הזדבר

עליהם זו על כשרות ישראל והיות ליד ימינם של הגאון, המסדרם

סדר הלך הגאון. כשרות וכו׳ המסורת באלפך הם מסורות

גדולה לעשות תיקונים וסדרים וזכית לזכות את בני

ישראל על ידי כשרות בסגנון שנגרם על ידי גדולי המסורות

לכן זכית גם עכשיו לזכות את בני ישראל את יסודות

הכשרות והסדרים שצריכים להבדיל בין הטמא והטהור

ובין הנאכלת ובין שאינה נאכלת.

ויהי רצון שתזכה מחיל אל חיל לזכות את ישראל

אמן.
ידידו המוקירו ומכבדו כערכו הרם

אלי׳ שוויי

AN APPROBATION – מכתב ברכה

CONGREGATION
BETH TEFILO EMANUEL TIKVAH
24225 GREENFIELD — 559-5022

RES. 15558 GEORGE WASHINGTON
SOUTHFIELD, MICHIGAN 48075
557-6828

הרב אליעזר לעווין
Rabbi Leizer Levin

ב"ה

חתני היקר הרב הגאון ר' יעקב הלוי ליפשיץ נ"י
[illegible] ניו־יארק אמר לי, שבדעתו לטובת
[illegible] בעניני כשרות להפיץ מעינותיו חוצה
לסדר ספר בשם "הכשרות" לברר כמה ענינים
[illegible] הלכה עפ"י שו"ע [illegible]
[illegible] התורה כל ימיו [illegible]
[illegible] פוסק,
[illegible] הנזכרים [illegible]
[illegible] יום יום [illegible] הספר הזה,
[illegible] שאתן לו הסכמתי [illegible]
[illegible] הענינים. השי"ת יעזור לו שיצליח
[illegible] הקדש,
[illegible]
הרב אליעזר לוין [illegible]

AN APPROBATION – מכתב ברכה

RAV ZACHARIAH GELLEY
162 BENNETT AVENUE
NEW YORK, N.Y. 10040

רב זכרי' געללעי
אב"ד דק"ק קהל עדת ישורון
נוא יארק נ"י

ב"ה

החיים ברכה ושלום לכבוד מוהר"ר יעקב הלוי ליפשיץ שליט"א
ור"ה של ביהכ"נ בית יוסף מאנסי

את יקרת מנחתו עם הקונטרסים וגליונות בעניני-כשרות, ואיסור והיתר
שכ"ת להדפיסם ולהפיצם לתועלת הרבים קיבלתי לנכון.

באמת דבר גדול עשה כת"ר לחבר חיבור כזה שהוא מלא אומן מלאכת
מחשבת בכי עבודה. של כמה שנים שנכתב בלשון ברור וצח שיבינו בו
היסודות שעליהם בנוים יסודי הכשרות, וע"י זה יבא תיקון בענינים
ענינים אלו אשר כל קדושת עם ישראל תלוי בזה. וכבר אמרו חז"ל
ביומא. "לא תטמאו בהם ונטמאתם" אם מטמאים אתם בה סופכם
ליטמא בה, כי המאכלות האסורות מכניסים טומאה ממש בלבו ובנפשו
של אדם עד שקדושתו של המקום ב"ה מסתלקת ומתרחקת ממנו והמאכלות
האסורות יתרות בזה על כל האיסורין כיון שהם נכנסים בגופו של אדם
ממש ונעשה בשר מבשרו. (לשונו של מסילת ישרים)

שמחתי לשמוע מכת"ר שהודעני להקדיש את ספרו על שמו של מוהר"ר
ר' יוסף ברייער זצ"ל רב ואב"ד ומייסד קהילתינו הק' קהל עדת ישורון
עם כל מוסדותיה ובפרט מוסדות הכשרות אשר מוה"ג זצ"ל פעל גדולות
בזה במדינתינו אשר כלנו נהנים מהגנתו, וכת"ר היה קשור אליו מאוד
וגם היה משגיח שיעורים בענינים אלו בבית מדרשו מזה שבע שנים.

ויה"א כיון שזכותו הגדול של הרב זצ"ל יעמוד לו שספרו
יתקבל ברצון, ומגלגלין זכות ע"י זכאי ויתברך בכל מילי דמיטב הוא
ובני ביתו וכל הנלווים אליו

בברכת ידידו

זכרי' געללעי

Publisher's Preface

Since time immemorial, kashruth observance was prime barometer of a Jewish family's commitment to Judaism. That has not changed. What *has* changed is the complexity of kashruth, which has undergone striking change, along with much else in modern life.

Our grandmothers would not dream of using meat that was not soaked and salted with their own hands in their own kitchens; our granddaughters have never seen a salting board. Not too many generations ago, all food was prepared in the kitchen; today most of it is processed before it is brought into the home. In the "good old days" we could take a short walk and see every ingredient as it was produced; today our components may come from several continents and contain chemical additives that few of us can even pronounce.

The result is that basic kashruth observance is no longer the simple task it once was. Coupled with this is widespread confusion about many aspects of the kashruth industry, both halachic and technical. Because of the complexity of kashruth in modern times, there is more today that the kosher consumer should know and understand than ever before. And certainly it is no less important.

The Sages (*Yoma* 39b) teach that the eating of non-kosher food has a harmful effect on the Jewish soul, even if it was done unintentionally. Even if it is absolutely necessary to employ a gentile wet nurse for a Jewish baby, we are enjoined to ensure that she eat only kosher food. Clearly, the nurture provided by non-kosher food is spiritually harmful even to an innocent infant (*Yoreh Deah* 81:7). Of course, every sin must be avoided, but a sin that is absorbed into the body, like non-kosher food, is far worse than one that is done with the hands; one is internalized while the other remains external. Consequently, despite the prolifer-ating and bewildering number of kashruth supervision services, the seriousness of kashruth observance places an obligation on Jews to know far more than package labels can tell them. Even the halachic scholar needs help in applying his knowledge to the reality of the modern market place.

The Jewish public is fortunate, therefore, that a man of the experience and stature of Rabbi Yacov Lipschutz undertook to write this book. Rabbi Lipschutz is the scion of a distinguished Lithuanian rabbinic family. He has been a kashruth administrator and supervisor for a quarter-century. In the process he has gained vast knowledge about modern food technology and the arcane science of food additives.

This is *not* a book on how to keep a kosher kitchen in ten easy lessons. But it *is* a book that will educate untold numbers of consumers — scholars and laymen, men and women — on the underlying principles on which the laws and practice of kashruth are based. The second section of the book contains a list of a hundred ingredients and additives, including their derivation, purpose, and whether or not they require kashruth supervision. An appendix provides the most complete up-to-date lists of properly-scaled and non-kosher fish available anywhere. The list was prepared especially for this book by Dr. James W. Atz, Curator Emeritus of the department of ichthyology of the American Museum of Natural History.

We are confident that this book will be acknowledged as a valuable addition to every home library. It should be read and re-read, and then kept handy for reference. Especially in this age of educated consumerism, this is the book that finally enables every Jew to become an educated *kosher* consumer.

Rabbi Meir Zlotowitz / Rabbi Nosson Scherman

Acknowledgments

Our Torah tell us that (בראשית ב:יח) — לא טוב היות האדם לבדו. Life's most lasting and meaningful benefits are attained together with others. The author is grateful to his colleagues: Rabbi Yitzchok Chinn and Rabbi Moshe Mendel Simon, Mr. Barry Eizik and Mr. Milton Wein, for their wise counsel.

To the members of industry who readily made available their libraries and resources, and who generously extended their assistance my thanks to: Dr. James Atz; Messrs. Dieter and Klaus Bauer; Benjamin Brecher; Neil Genschaft; Jerold Krupnick; Alan, Arnold, Bruce and Steven Manheimer; and Selwyn, Seymour and Wilfred Weiss.

For their expert editorial work and constant encouragement I am grateful to: Mr. Yaakov Kornreich; the General Editors of Mesorah Publications, Rabbi Meir Zlotowitz and Rabbi Nosson Scherman; Rabbi Hersh Goldwurm and Rabbi Avie Gold. Their erudite comments and constructive critique were invaluable in the preparation of the manuscript and book.

To Rabbi Sheah Brander whose much-heralded graphics mastery transformed information into an attractive, useful book, I am deeply grateful. My appreciation is extended as well to the typesetters and office personnel of Mesorah Publications for their unfailing efficiency and courtesy.

To my wife, Tzipora, for her painstaking attention to detail and constant support; to my dear parents, Rabbi and Mrs. Benjamin Lipschutz, Fall River, Mass.; Rabbi Leizer Levin, Detroit, Mich.; Rebetzin Sarah Wachtfogel, Jerusalem; to my brother, Irving, my brother-in-law and sister, Mr. and Mrs. Fred Weinberg; to all my children and grandchildren; to the officers, members and friends of my congregation, K'hal Beth Joseph, Monsey, whose closeness and loyalty have been a constant inspiration — May G-d bless them all with the rewards of a rich and long Torah-imbued life.

יהא רעוא דאימא מילתא דתתקבל
וה׳ יצילני מהשגיאות
Y.L.

Table of Contents

Kashruth

The essence of *Am Yisroel*, the Jewish people, is its spirituality and holiness, that within the body of the Jew there resides a holy and eternal soul. Each *mitzvah* serves as a constant reminder of this existence. Therefore, even a commonplace function such as physical nourishment, when properly fulfilled, is sacred in nature, and sanctifies the human body. Conversely the consumption of forbidden foods defiles the holy spirit, and its sanctity is injured. This injury reduces the Jewish capacity to reap the full spiritual rewards of Torah and its fathomless depths. The result of eating forbidden foods is referred to by the Talmudic Sages as *timtum halev* – damaging the heart's ability to fully comprehend.

It is therefore not surprising that the observance of kashruth is a mainstay of Jewish existence and Jewish identity. Throughout Jewish history, the true Jewish soul endured the pressures of persecution rather than eat of forbidden foods, and maintained the precious *mitzvos* of kashruth. To the dedicated Jew there exists a religious force so deeply embedded in the soul that even the most delectable serving of milk and meat or flesh of the swine becomes abominable and physically revolting.

To the Jew, the observance of kashruth is not viewed as a restriction preventing him from partaking of culinary pleasure. The affirmation that kashruth gives to his spiritual qualities is the eternal pleasure that true Torah observance brings to life. Just as the faithful Jew does not conceive of lighting a cigarette at the Shabbos table, so too, is the very thought of eating of the forbidden completely foreign to him.

Down through the centuries many have attributed kashruth to either hygienic or social separation purposes. However, these extraneous motivations fail to stand up before the onslaught of human temptations, especially those of our contemporary society. Only when the Jew observes kashruth as a matter of faith does his commitment permeate his entire life, home, and surroundings, bringing to him the meaning of the message of the Almighty's teachings.

What is more evident than the multifold tragedy of the American Jewish home — families that are bereft of the moral dignity which was for generations the axiom of being a Jew? In homes where the self-discipline of Torah and kashruth was not practiced in their entirety the gates were left open for other, alien practices to enter and erode the Jewish way of life.

We hope that this work will both inspire and educate, inspiring readers of all backgrounds, uninitiated as well as learned, to the desired goals of a truly religious Torah life. If we bring such fortune to the reader we shall consider our work blessed, and our labors a success.

Meat

⁓§ The Kosher Species

Animals*

The Torah identifies the animals whose flesh may be eaten as ruminants (i.e., cud-chewing animals) whose hooves are split. A ruminant's stomach consists of four chambers (see illustration, p.28). They are: the rumen (*keres*); the reticulum (*beis hakosos*) from which the food is redigested upward; the omasum (*hemsas*) to which it then returns; and the abomasum (*kaivah*). The cud then passes from the chambers to the duodenum. In addition to the chambers of the stomach the animal must be cloven-hoofed,

* The laws of this section are discussed in *Yoreh Deah* 79.

as identified in *Leviticus* 11:3 and *Deuteronomy* 14:6: "Among the animals you may eat any one that has cloven hoofs and that brings up its cud."

Some authorities point out that the physical appearance of the animal is of itself insufficient to establish it as kosher. It must also be accepted by tradition as one of the ten species enumerated in *Deuteronomy* 14:4-5. The Talmud explains that since there are far more non-kosher animals than kosher, the Torah enumerates the animals that are kosher.

Rambam (*Forbidden Foods* 1:8) states: "There are not in the entire universe any animals that are permitted to be eaten except for the ten species enumerated in the Torah." Based on this ruling animals of the other species that appear to have the kosher physical identification are neverthelesss to be excluded from the kosher species, since they are not among the types mentioned in the Torah.

Fowl*

In the case of fowl, the Torah enumerates the non-kosher species, since these are fewer in number than those species which are kosher. "These are the flying animals that you must avoid. Since they are to be avoided, do not eat any . . ." (*Leviticus* 11:12-19).

The Torah does not describe the physical characteristics of these fowl, and therefore, it is the established religious tradition based on the *Shulchan Aruch* (Code of Law) that the physical characteristics that have been found to be unique to the forbidden fowl cannot alone be the determining factor to identify the kosher status of birds. Only those that through the generations have been by tradition positively identified as kosher may be accepted as a kosher species.

---

* The laws of this section are discussed in *Yoreh Deah* 82.

It is not surprising to find that the origins of many species of fowl are the subject of Talmudic responsa, and their kosher status remains in doubt. Among them:

(1) the quail and the pheasant, which many scholars maintain are not related to the quail and pheasant mentioned in the Torah;

(2) the guinea hen and the peacock, which many scholars regard as non-kosher; and

(3) various species of wild geese, which many scholars regard as unrelated to domestic kosher geese.

At one time the status of the domestic turkey was questioned. In this case Torah authorities established the bird as kosher, and this tradition is followed universally.

Not only is the meat of a non-kosher animal or bird forbidden, but its milk and eggs are forbidden as well. Such gourmet food items as quail or pheasant eggs are non-kosher. Similarly in parts of the world where the domestic poultry is of unknown variety, Jews must abstain from the meat and eggs of these birds until competent authorities establish that the species is kosher.

Shechitah (Kosher Slaughter)*

The flesh of kosher animals may be eaten only after *shechitah* has been performed. The Torah describes this *mitzvah* briefly in *Deuteronomy* 12:21: "You shall slaughter your cattle and flock." Although the Torah states it very briefly and without elaboration, the details of this *mitzvah* were taught by Moshe Rabbeinu (Moses), and transmitted orally, until transcribed in the Mishnah and Talmud in great detail.

* The laws of this section are discussed in *Yoreh Deah* 1,18,20-25.

The *mitzvah* requires that in animals both the trachea (windpipe) and esophagus (foodpipe) be severed by cutting in the prescribed area (*zevichah*). In fowl it is sufficient that either one of these be cut. The cut must sever either the entire or the major portion of the organ, and must be performed with continuous strokes, without pressure or hesitation.

The blade used must be sharp and perfectly free of any nicks or imperfections on the cutting edge. These requirements are prescribed in the five basic disqualifications of *shechitah.*

(1) *Sh'hiyah* — hesitation. The cut must be made with continuous strokes. Even a moment's hesitation at any point in the *shechitah* renders it invalid and the meat non-kosher.

(2) *Hagramah* — cutting out of the proper area. The trachea and the esophagus may not be cut above or below the specific area proscribed for *shechitah.* When cut outside these areas, the meat is non-kosher. Traditionally, therefore, *shechitah* is performed towards the center of the neck to eliminate the possibility of error. After the *shechitah* the cut is to be examined by the *shochet* (slaughterer), to guarantee that both the trachea and the esophagus have been properly severed.

(3) *Drasah* — pressing. No pressure may be applied while the *shechitah* is performed; the cut must be made solely by the sharpness of the moving blade. Even placing a finger on the blade renders the *shechitah* unfit.

(4) *Ikur* — tearing. The trachea and esophagus must be severed by cutting, and may not be torn; therefore the blade used must be flawless, since any imperfections, nicks, and chips would tear the organ as it cuts. Before the *shechitah,* it is necessary to examine the

knife carefully. Traditionally the *shochet* cautiously runs his fingernail over the blade in order to detect any imperfections.

(5) *Chaladah* – cutting while the knife is under cover. The *shechitah* is valid only when the blade is fully exposed during the cutting. Any covering – whether it be cloth, or the hair, wool or feathers of the animal or fowl – invalidates the *shechitah*. When *shechitah* is performed on sheep, particular caution is necessary to insure that the blade remains fully exposed at all times, and is not covered by the animal's wool. Many authorities require that the neck area of sheep be shorn, while others permit grasping the wool so that the skin is bared, enabling the blade to remain exposed during *shechitah*.

Before *shechitah* is performed, it is necessary to be sure that the animal's neck area is clean, free of mud, pebbles, dirt and sand, that could impair the *shechitah* process. Unless the neck is properly hosed down it is possible that the cutting blade will be nicked by such foreign matter, or that the pebbles, etc., may impede the knife's cutting motion, and be considered an interruption.

The entire *shechitah* process is one that requires a well-trained individual possessing skill, piety and expertise. Traditionally, a *shochet* must receive *kabbalah*, a document from a Rabbinic authority testifying that he is learned in the laws of *shechitah*, and trustworthy in its performance. The *shochet* performs a most critical function that is basic to communal kashruth observance, and must maintain the standards of piety and skill worthy of his responsibility.

◆§ B'dikah (Examination) and "Glatt" Kosher*

Consumers are often confused by the use of the term *"glatt kosher"* as opposed to "kosher" in describing the kashruth standards of meat and other products. Although the use of the term *"glatt"* is not a guarantee of kashruth authenticity unless properly attested to, it is commonly used to indicate an extra degree of precaution and kashruth standards; however, this use is unrelated to the true origins of the term *"glatt."*

From our brief description of the basic laws of *shechitah,* we can appreciate the demanding requirements in both physical skill and religious dedication necessary to carry out the *shochet's* position of kashruth trust. Equal to this is the skill and piety demanded of the individual who will examine the animal's organs to verify its kashruth. It is from this examination that the word *"glatt"* is derived, as will be evident from the following discussion.

We are all familiar with the term *"treifah"* (often shortened to *treif*), which is commonly used to mean any food that is not kosher. However, the specific meaning of *treifah* is "torn." The Torah passage (*Exodus* 22:30) from which this word is borrowed reads: "And you shall be a sanctified people to me. And the flesh that has been torn (*treifah*) in the field may not be eaten, and should be cast to the dogs." The phrase "the flesh that has been torn in the field" implies two kinds of *treifah:* (1) meat that has been torn from a live animal and is therefore forbidden; (2) animals whose organs have been damaged by being torn or distressed.

The injuries and diseases that render an animal forbidden

---

* The laws of this section are discussed in *Yoreh Deah* 29-60.

are defects that affect all the major organs, which are either missing, perforated, torn, poisoned, broken or injured in a fall. Included in these are the brain, heart, spinal column, jaw, esophagus, crop (in fowl), lungs, trachea, liver, gall bladder, spleen, kidney, womb, intestines, omasum, abomasum, rumen, reticulum, legs, ribs, and hide.

Under normal conditions the majority of animals do not suffer from diseases or injuries in all the above-mentioned organs. Therefore it is not necessary to examine them after *shechitah* unless there is an indication that injury or disease is present. Pus, blood, swelling, malformations and palsied actions of the animal are a few of the signs indicating that further examination of the affected organ is necessary.

In countries where specific animal diseases are common in fowl or cattle, the organs that may be affected must be examined.

For example, in the United States it is not necessary to examine the legs of chickens, but in Israel and Mediterranean countries a variety of diseases affect the legs of fowl, and their legs require examination. In the United States it is customary to examine the intestines of fowl, since many birds have been found to have abscesses in that area.

The Lungs*

Since the lungs of all animals are commonly affected by defects which may render them *treifah* it is necessary for the lungs to be examined before the animal can be confirmed as kosher. This examination is referred to as the *b'dikah* (examination).

[In the United States the lungs of fowl are not prone to defects and require no examination. However, in countries where it is known that the fowl are afflicted, the lungs must

* The laws of this section are discussed in *Yoreh Deah* 35-39.

be examined and found to be free of defect. Only those birds whose lungs are found to be in perfect condition are accepted as kosher.]

The lungs are first examined before they are removed from the chest cavity. The examiner (*bodek*) carefully opens the diaphragm and inserts his hand into the cavity, passing his hand over the lobes of the lung, at which time he determines whether or not there are any adhesions on the lungs, and whether or not the lungs are properly formed.

The lungs are then carefully removed from the body cavity and examined once again externally. This examination will confirm that each lung is free of any defect. When this is found to be so, the lungs are described not only as kosher, but by the Hebrew term *chalak* (perfectly smooth) or *glatt* in Yiddish. This kosher status will have been established by both an internal examination (*b'dikas p'nim*) and an external examination (*b'dikas chutz*).

Since the term *"glatt"* in reference to examination of the lungs means perfectly free of blemish, it has been turned into a colloquial term that refers to a kashruth standard that is without question. Thus, the term *"glatt"* as used with reference to foods other than meat is a misnomer that has achieved popular acceptance.

Meat may be kosher, even if it is non-*glatt,* meaning that there are adhesions found on the lungs. If these adhesions can be peeled from the surface of the affected lung without perforating the lung, the animal is kosher, though not *glatt* kosher. The process of peeling an adhesion must be done with great skill and care. Blood in the adhesion indicates a perforation and the animal is not kosher. After the adhesion is peeled from the lung, the lung is inflated and the area that was peeled is placed in water. This will show whether or not there are any perforations. If any bubbling occurs, it indicates that the lung was perforated, and the animal is *treifah.* Only when the lungs are found to be sound is the meat kosher, although not *glatt.* This process is referred to as *klipas hasirchos* (the peeling of adhesions); and is permitted according to the Ashkenazic European tradition. The Sephardic tradition restricts this practice, and only *chalak* or *glatt* is permissible. Since the practice of *klipas hasirchos* is a matter of diverse opinions, the meat of *glatt* animals is always preferred.

Veal and Lamb

The Ashkenazic tradition of *klipas hasirchos* is limited to fully grown cattle. The procedure may not be performed on the lungs of calves and lambs. The lungs of these animals must always be *glatt.*

Under normal conditions young livestock are not as prone as older cattle to diseases affecting the lungs. Adhesions are therefore not too common. However, increased consumer demand for tender, flavorful "white veal" has produced a type of veal that is derived from "nature-fed" calves. These calves are raised under conditions that confine the animals to small spaces, limiting their movement and their diet. They are milk fed, in order to make their meat tender and light in color. Despite the fact that these "nature calves" receive regular doses of antibiotic medication to keep them disease free, as a result of their confinement and poor diet, most are found to have developed lung adhesions; and are therefore *treifah.*

Additionally, lambs often present problems during the *shechitah* when the wool is fully grown in the neck area. Measures must be taken so that the hair does not interfere with the *shechitah* — (see "Shechitah").

At certain times of the year many lambs are afflicted with intestinal diseases causing abscesses on their intestines. When this occurs, the intestines must be examined to determine that there are no perforations and that the intestines are intact.

◈ Nikur / Traboring (De-veining)*

Blood Vessels

Many know that kosher meat must undergo *nikur* and be *trabored,* but most people are puzzled as to the precise purpose and procedure of this process. The Hebrew word *nikur* and its Yiddish equivalent, *trabor,* mean to dig out; in the case of meat, it refers to the requirement for excision of the veins, arteries, and forbidden fats.

In addition to the blood that would be extracted by the koshering-salting process, blood remains pooled in major arteries of the animal, and, if left intact, this blood will not be extracted by salting. Therefore these arteries must be severed and exposed before koshering, in order to permit the free flow of blood from them by soaking and salting. Rather than merely severing each of these blood vessels, it is traditional that they be removed completely from the neck through the shoulder and foreleg, the ribs, the brisket, the navel area, and the tongue.

After the slaughter, a large pool of blood remains in the heart. Before being koshered, therefore, the heart must be opened to permit the blood to flow out. (In some communities it is traditional to avoid use of the heart for mystical reasons unrelated to kashruth.) The membrane of the brains and sweetbreads (neck glands), which are popular entree foods, must be removed before koshering. The brain membrane consists of many blood vessels, while that of the glands is so saturated with the *shechitah* blood that it too must be peeled away.

---

* The laws of this section are discussed in *Yoreh Deah* 65.

All clotted blood found on meat or poultry must be either scraped or rinsed away before koshering. Blood blotches on the meat or poultry should be cut open, so that, during soaking and salting, the blood will flow from them. When consumers find wings or legs of poultry that are bloodied, this may indicate an injury that occurred before *shechitah* and, depending upon the area, the bird may have become *treifah.* Such injuries must be shown to an expert in matters of *treifah* for consultation and decision. This is true of already koshered chickens, as well, since the internal joints, etc., are not visible at the time of the koshering.

Poultry do not require the excising of any blood vessels with the exception of the blood vessel in the neck, which must be either severed or removed. Once the head is removed this blood vessel has been severed and is ready for koshering. Nevertheless, many customarily either severe it again or remove it. It is also traditional to clip the wing tips and to cut the leg at the knee joint (shank). This enhances the flow of blood from the blood vessels.

This painstaking kashruth process of preparing meat for koshering requires training, skill and piety. The consumer must be able to rely on the religious responsibility of the individuals involved and upon their dedication to kashruth.

Chailev (Forbidden fats)

The Torah forbids the eating of *chailev,* the restricted fats, of animals that are eligible for the Temple's sacrificial service: cattle, sheep or goats. This prohibition is stated in the verse (*Leviticus* 7:23): "You shall not eat the fats of the ox, sheep or goat." Not included in this prohibition are species of animals not fit for the sacrifices and wild animals, e.g., antelope, deer, gazelle, etc.

The Talmud specifies the location of the forbidden fats as the fat of the stomachs (omasum, abomasum, and rumen).

Ruminants have four stomachs which are covered with a fatty watery membrane, the peritoneum. This membrane is included in the *chailev* of this prohibition (see diagram).

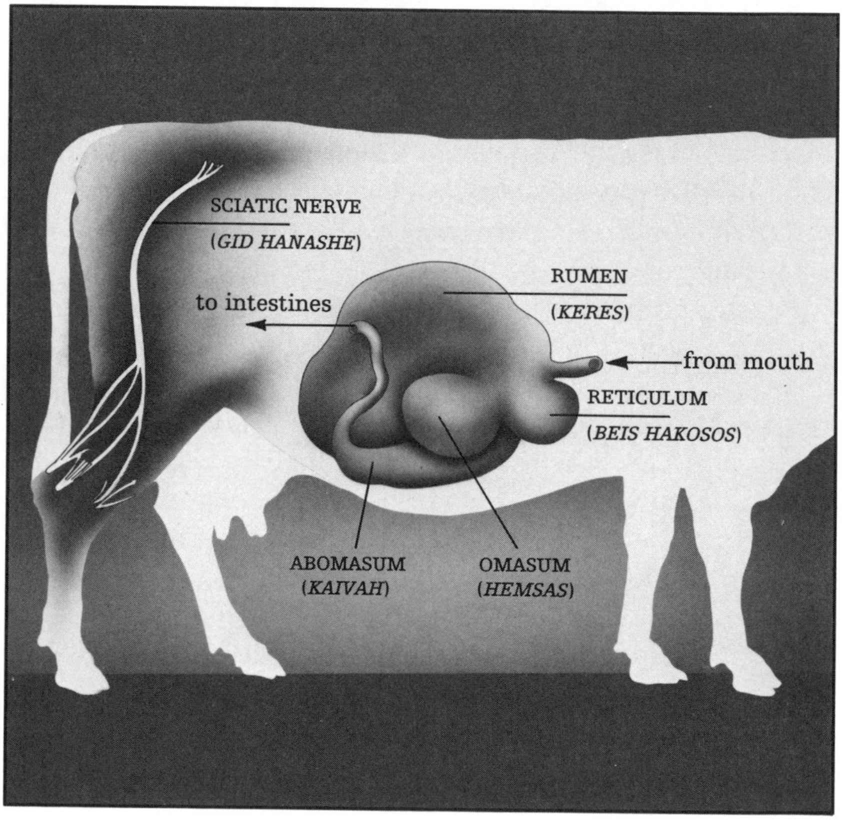

Also in the category of *chailev* are the fat covering the kidneys and body cavity over the hind legs or the loins, and the diaphragm upon which the liver rests. The diaphragm is the midriff wall separating the intestinal digestive organs from the respiratory organs, heart and lungs. It has become traditional in most of the western world to limit the use of kosher meat to those parts that are in the respiratory area of the animal (front quarter), which extends to the twelfth rib, at which point the carcass is split.

There are several organs in the intestinal area that are

commonly used and require removal of fats:

(a) The liver, which lies on the intestinal wall adjacent to the stomach, must be scraped clean of the fats attached to it.

(b) The membrane and cords of the spleen, referred to in Yiddish as "miltz," are removed.

(c) Both the membrane and all the fats in which the meat is embedded are removed from the hanging tender (a muscle which hangs beyond the diaphragm near the kidneys).

(d) Forbidden fats and cords are removed from "oxtails" at the point where it is attached to the animal.

(e) The intestines are often used as the casing for such popular foods as stuffed derma (kishka) or as natural casings for frankfurters. These intestines must be scraped clean of all forbidden fats and membranes.

(f) In the area of the lower midsection, the navel, there are several areas which require removal of the membranes, fats and cords that extend into it from the rear. Included in it are the membranes covering the skirt steaks. Fats and connecting tissue are removed from the meat of the navel area, commonly referred to as the plate or pastrami piece. (Kosher consumers often complain that, in comparison to other koshered meats, skirt steaks are very salty. This is because this small cut is individually koshered only after the outer-skin membrane is removed. The salt easily permeates the meat, and even after thorough rinsing, it remains salty. Some butchers recommend soaking the koshered steak for several hours before broiling to eliminate the salty flavor.)

Since the meat of the hindquarter of the animal is not sold as kosher in the United States, this eliminates the need for the extremely tedious process of excising the forbidden *chailev* in the hindquarter and the *gid hanashe* (sciatic nerve), which is described in *Genesis* 32:33: "Therefore the children of Israel shall not eat the *gid hanashe*;" which comes from the rear of the spinal column and branches down through the entire hind leg. (See diagram above, page 28.)

The removal of the forbidden veins and fats is a painstaking task; and the entire koshering process requires a high degree of religious responsibility, anatomical knowledge, skill and training. The selection of a kosher butcher should be based primarily on these professional criteria.

Koshering Meat

Blood*

The Torah forbids the blood of all animals and fowl, whether wild or domestic, and whether the blood is in liquid form or is part of the muscle, tissue, bone or fat. "You shall not eat any blood, whether it be fowl or beast" (*Leviticus* 7:26).

The blood of fish and insects is not included in this prohibition, but the blood of forbidden species of fish and insects may not be eaten, since it is the product of non-kosher species. The varieties of blood that are permissible may be consumed only when the origin of the blood is obvious. This restriction avoids creating the appearance that a transgression has taken place, when in fact it has not. This is referred to as *mar'is ha'ayin.* For this reason it is permitted to swallow one's own blood (such as in cases where the gums are bleeding), since the consumption of this blood is not visible.

The blood of flesh, bone and muscle is forbidden only once it flows from the tissue. Raw, kosher-slaughtered

* The laws of this section are discussed in *Yoreh Deah* 67-69.

meat in its original state may be eaten after it has been rinsed free of any surface blood. However, the veins and arteries must be removed, since the blood which remains in these blood vessels is forbidden even in the raw state. When meat is cooked, placed in hot water or allowed to soak for a period of twenty-four hours the blood flows from the meat, is re-absorbed and the meat becomes permanently non-kosher. The extraction of the blood from meat is commonly referred to as "koshering" the meat, simply because it is only after this procedure that the meat is free of any forbidden blood.

Meat that has been ground before koshering may not be consumed raw, since it is impossible to rinse each particle; nor may it be koshered, since the particles can no longer be properly soaked and salted.

Many times, there is still a flow of juices from the meat after the koshering. This is not a matter of concern, for once the meat has been properly koshered all the forbidden blood has been removed, and the juices that flow thereafter are permissible.

The procedure for extracting the blood from meat may be done by either broiling or salting. Liver, due to its natural composition, may only be koshered by broiling.

Koshering by Salting*

Before beginning the salting process of meat, the necessary equipment should be prepared: soaking pails, a grate or board on which to place the meat, drip pans or sink area into which the blood may flow freely, water and "koshering salt." In addition the entire procedure should first be reviewed with competent authorities and personally observed before attempting to kosher meat.

---

* The laws of this section are discussed in *Yoreh Deah* 69.

The meat must first be rinsed free of any blood that is on the surface, for each time meat is cut it is assumed that blood has come to the surface. On the meat of the neck area, where the blood congeals due to the bleeding of the *shechitah,* it is necessary to scrape the blood from the flesh before the rinsing. When clots or bruise marks are found elsewhere in the flesh — indicating that blood has concentrated in that place — these should be cut and rinsed, so that when salted the salt will extract the additional blood fluid which has gathered in the tissue.

After thorough rinsing of all exposed surfaces with water, the meat should be soaked for a period of one half hour. This additional soaking is done in order to sufficiently soften the meat and prepare it for the extraction of the blood. (Since the soaking of meat contains blood, it is customary that the tub or bucket used for the soaking should be set aside exclusively for this purpose.)

The water used for rinsing and soaking the meat should neither be very cold nor hot. Cold water stiffens the meat, making the tissues unsuitable for blood extraction. Hot water causes the blood to flow and be reabsorbed in the tissue, and it can no longer be koshered. To guarantee that the koshering procedure is properly effective, it is common practice to exercise caution and to use water at a temperature no lower than 50° F or higher than 80° F.

Because of this, in kosher poultry plants, heated water is never used in the plucking or defeathering process, since the use of hot water would make the birds unfit for koshering.

When koshering meat that has been frozen, it must be fully thawed before the soaking, salting and koshering, since these procedures are not effective when the meat is frozen.

When a small section of the meat is not submerged during the soaking process, and the protruding surface has been thoroughly rinsed, authorities point out that it may be assumed that the submerged portion absorbed enough water to sufficiently soften the entire piece of meat.

After the soaking, the meat is rinsed again. This rinsing washes off the soak-water and any blood that may have remained in the residue of that water. The water is then permitted to drip from the meat, in order to ensure that surface water will not dissolve the salt sprinkled on the meat. Nor may the surface be completely dry when salted, since the salt would not be effective when the meat is dry.

The meat is to be covered with salt that is coarse enough for the granules to perform the extraction, and not dissolve on the surface. Therefore powdered and finely granulated salts are not fit for the koshering process. Also unsuitable is salt that is excessively thick, e.g., rock salt or pellets, since these do not dissolve and penetrate the surface there is no extraction. A flake type salt of medium coarseness is most suitable for the koshering purpose, and is commonly referred to as "kosher salt."

Salt should be sprinkled on the meat, completely covering the entire exposed surface of the meat. Any flaps or cuts in the meat must be covered on all sides, as well. The same is true when koshering poultry. Both the surface facing the cavity and the outer surface must be entirely covered with salt. Once the surface has been thoroughly covered with salt it will effectively extract the blood (kosher the meat) regardless of the size and thickness of the piece of meat being koshered. The meat must then be placed in a position where it can drain freely, on a grate or inclined smooth surface that permits the free flow of blood. While undergoing the koshering process, salted cuts of meat may be piled one on top of the other, as long as the meat is laying on a grate or smooth, inclined surface. This is permitted because while the blood is being extracted from a cut of meat, that cut will not absorb the blood being extracted from the other pieces. At no time may the meat be placed on a flat surface that is either not perforated or not on an incline. This would inhibit the free flow of the blood from the meat and would be non-kosher.

When a grate is used, the pan underneath it should be deep enough so that the weight of the meat does not press the grate into the bloody brine that accumulates in the pan. Shallow pans are unsuitable for the koshering process, since the weight of the meat could press the grate into the pan, making the meat non-kosher. If the grate is placed in a sink or tub the same precaution must be taken to insure that there is adequate space to prevent the grate from being depressed onto the surface on the brine. The tubs and boards used for salting meat should be used exclusively for this purpose, and not be used for other foods.

The meat is to remain salted for a one-hour period. In instances of difficult circumstances, alternate time periods may be established, under the guidance of competent authorities.

It is essential that the salted meat be placed in an area where it will not be splashed with water, or come in contact with other foods. The water causes the salt to become ineffective, and other foods coming into contact with meats being koshered would absorb the non-kosher extracted blood.

After the salting period, the meat must be thoroughly rinsed of all salt, either by heavily rinsing the meat three times, or by three thorough soakings, each time in clean water. This triple rinsing and soaking removes all the salt, blood and rinse-water that have come in contact with the forbidden blood on the surface.

Koshering by Broiling*

Besides by soaking and salting, blood is also extracted from meat by broiling. The intensity of the heat extracts the blood from the tissue. This process is the only method by which liver may be koshered. It is also invaluable for individuals on salt-restricted diets. For many the thought of kosher-broiling creates an image of splattered stoves and ranges, and they are discouraged from attempting to kosher-broil liver or other meats. However, with careful preparation and attention to detail, when done with proper utensils, kosher-broiling is no more difficult than general food preparation.

This chapter will introduce the necessary guidelines and practical methods for the kosher-broiling process. It is advisable before attempting to kosher meat by either the salting or broiling method that some firsthand experience be gained by observing the procedure being carried out, and by having an experienced individual present when koshering for the first time. The entire procedure should be reviewed with a competent authority for explanation and clarification.

Although the intensity of the heat extracts the blood from the tissue and removes any blood on the surface, as an added precaution it is traditional to rinse the meat with cold water before broiling. It is also traditional to sprinkle a few grains of salt on the meat to aid in the extraction. When salt was not used, either by error or because the meat was being prepared for individuals who are salt restricted, the broiled meat is kosher. The same is true if the meat was not rinsed before broiling.

When frozen meat is to be kosher-broiled it must first be thawed out before koshering.

The fire used for broiling may be from any heat source,

---

* The laws of this section are discussed in *Yoreh Deah* 73, 76.

e.g., a flame, electric coils, coals, etc. This heat source may be either above or below the meat. (Authorities maintain that microwaves are not a flame and are not to be used for kosher-broiling.) Meat that is to be kosher-broiled is to be placed on a rack or spit. The extracted blood must flow from the meat unimpeded. Since the meat may not lay in the extracted blood, the broiling grills commonly found in residential ovens are not suitable for the kosher-broiling process, because they permit the meat to lay in the blood which gathers in the grooves of the grill. Screens and grids with narrow holes are easily clogged during broiling, and are therefore not suitable for koshering. Most suitable is a grid whose parallel wires are spaced far enough apart so that they cannot be clogged, yet close enough together (approximately one half inch) to prevent the slices of meat from falling into the pan. These types of grids are available in most houseware departments. The typical outdoor barbecue grill fired by coal or gas flame may also be used for kosher-broiling. The grid should be placed on a pan that is deep enough to insure that the meat lies well above the drippings. Cookie sheets are too shallow for this purpose. It is best to use a baking pan that is approximately one and a half inch or more in depth. This insures that regardless of the weight of the meat it will always rest clear of the extracted blood.

The blood and all the drippings during the broiling are non-kosher, and the pan used to catch the drippings becomes non-kosher as well, and may not be used for other foods. In order to avoid cleaning and scraping the pan some housekeepers line it with aluminum foil, and merely discard the foil after use. Others find it even more practical to use disposable aluminum pans.

It is traditional practice that the grid or spit used for kosher-broiling not be used for other foods unless it has been koshered by a flame under the guidance of a competent authority. If by oversight the grid was used for meat already koshered, expert guidance must be sought. When chicken livers are broiled, the grid should have slightly narrower spaces to prevent the small livers from slipping into the pan and becoming non-kosher. Some have improvised by using a mesh grate commonly found in houseware stores and designed for shredding vegetables. If the spaces of such a mesh are wide enough to permit the free flow of the blood, it may be used for kosher-broiling.

The meat should be left to broil until the entire piece is half-broiled. It is insufficient for the outside to be well done, and the inside to remain rare. Once the entire piece is half-broiled, the blood has been extracted, and the meat is kosher. The juices that continue to flow afterwards are permissible.

While the meat is broiling it is permissible to turn the meat over occasionally so that it will be evenly broiled. However, the meat should not be constantly turning during the koshering procedure. This too is a precaution to aid in the free flow of blood from the meat. If by mistake the meat was allowed to turn constantly, e.g., on a rotisserie, it is nevertheless kosher. When necessary, it is permitted to momentarily remove the meat from the fire, and then return it to broil until kosher. Several pieces of meat may be broiled together, and may come in contact with each other, since one piece of meat does not absorb the blood drippings of the next piece while its own blood is being extracted.

Due to the excessive amount of blood in the natural composition of liver, it should not be kosher-broiled together with other types of meat, since the flow of blood from liver is far greater than that of other meat. Nevertheless, if this was done in error, all the meats are kosher.

The knives, forks or prongs used to turn or cut the meat before it is half-broiled come in contact with the blood, and therefore should not be used for other foods, unless they are koshered under the guidance of a competent authority. In cases where this was not done, however, and inadvertently the utensils were used for other foods, a competent authority should be consulted.

After the meat is kosher-broiled, it is traditional to rinse the surface with cool water as a precautionary measure to wash off any residual blood on the surface. If the meat was not rinsed it is nevertheless kosher.

"Washed" Meat / Seventy-two Hours*

Many consumers are often puzzled by discussions of "washed meat" and the merits of its kosher status. Some purveyors may display signs saying "Meat Soaked and Salted Within 72 Hours," and designate separate shelves for "Washed Meat."

The principle of koshering meat by soaking and salting is that the salt will sufficiently act on the meat and extract the blood from the capillaries. During the post-Talmudic Gaonic period 4349 (589 C.E.) to 4798 (1038 C.E.), the Gaonic Sages ruled that after the first seventy-two hours following the slaughter, the blood has congealed in the capillaries to a point where it can no longer be assumed that the salting will completely extract it. From that point on, the meat can be koshered by broiling only, since the intensity of the heat is sufficient to extract all the blood.

Since the ruling of the Gaonic Sages requiring salting within seventy-two hours is due to the change in the condition of the blood, if the meat is soaked in water for approximately a half hour during the first seventy-two hours, the capillaries are sufficiently softened to be identi-

* The laws of this section are discussed in *Yoreh Deah* 69.

cal to those of fresh meat, and the meat may be koshered within the next seventy-two hours. This process may be repeated again if necessary.

There are those who state that only soaking will affect the blood vessels sufficiently to extend the koshering period. Other authorities maintain that a thorough rinsing of the meat is equally effective, and that it need not be soaked.

When the koshering period of meat has been extended by the rinse method it is referred to as "washed meat." This informs the consumer that the meat was koshered within seventy-two hours of a *rinsing.*

In later years the question arose as to the status of frozen meat, and whether it is subject to the ruling of the Gaonic Sages. Many authorities maintain that the Gaonic ruling is all inclusive, and frozen meat, too, must be koshered within seventy-two hours; while others are of the opinion that frozen meat is not affected and may be kosher-salted after it has been thawed.

Once the seventy-two-hour period has passed and the meat is koshered by broiling, it should not undergo further processing such as cooking, frying, etc. Some authorities maintain that liver, due to its natural composition, may be cooked or fried after it has been properly broiled. Others apply the same restriction to liver as well as to all other meats. If by error meat extended beyond the seventy-two hours was cooked after broiling, it is nevertheless kosher.

The seventy-two-hour restriction not only affects the koshering of meat, but its storage as well. Meat should not be kept unkoshered beyond the seventy-two-hour period since it is possible that, by error, the regular procedure of soaking and salting will be done at a time when it is no longer effective. However, liver is an exception to this rule, since broiling is the only koshering process used for liver, there is no fear that it will be salted and, therefore, there is no time limit on its storage.

Separation of Meat and Milk

◆§ The Torah Prohibition*

The prohibition of mixing milk and meat together is based upon the passage: "You shall not cook a kid in its mother's milk" (*Exodus* 23:19; 34:26; and *Deuteronomy* 14:21). This reference is meant to include not only a kid, but the meat and milk of all domestic animals. The Talmud further states that since this passage is repeated three times, each passage indicates a distinct prohibition. Therefore, it is derived that (a) it is forbidden to cook a mixture of

* The laws of this section are discussed in *Yoreh Deah* 87.

milk and meat of domestic animals; and if cooked (b) it may not be eaten; and (c) no benefit whatsoever may be derived from it. Since all use is restricted, it is forbidden to sell the cooked mixture, to give it as a gift, or to use it as animal feed. Therefore one must exercise caution in the use of pet foods and feeds produced from beef, veal or mutton, containing milk and processed by cooking. [The phrase "domestic animals" as used here is a technical term and refers to those animals that fall into the Torah classification of *behaimah;* the phrase "wild animals" (below) refers to those classified as *chayah.*]

In order to avoid any mistaken consumption of the forbidden cooked mixture, the Talmud extended the prohibition to restrict the eating of uncooked meat together with milk. They also extended it to the consumption of kosher fowl or wild animals with milk. Although uncooked meat with milk may not be eaten, the prohibition of these mixtures is only that they may not be *eaten*, but they may be used for other purposes. Mixtures of milk with the meat of wild animals or fowl may be cooked for non-kosher use.

The restriction of cooking milk with meat is a matter of lengthy responsa. Many maintain that cooking is a general term, and is meant to forbid frying and broiling as well. Others maintain that frying and broiling of the meat and milk mixture is not included. The degree of cooking forbidden by the Torah is a matter of discussion as well. Many authorities maintain that any heating of a meat and milk mixture is forbidden, even if the food remains raw. Others hold that unless the mixture is cooked until it is considered edible (approximately one-third cooked), there is no prohibition.

The prohibition of cooking milk and meat has far reaching effects, and such mixtures may not be cooked together even when the foods are to be eaten by non-Jews. This prohibits a Jewish worker in a non-kosher facility from cooking meats of kosher domestic animals with dairy products. When the foods themselves are not mixed, but the utensils are, it is forbidden to cook milk for non-kosher use in meat utensils that have been used to heat meat in the immediately preceding twenty-four-hour period, and vice-versa.

Milk after Meat*

As an extension of the prohibition against eating cooked milk-meat mixtures, even unmixed and uncooked milk and meat may not be eaten together. Furthermore a time period must elapse before one may eat dairy foods after having eaten meat. The nearly universal tradition for the duration of that time period is six hours. However, in some Western European communities a waiting period of three hours was customary. The time is measured from when the meat was last consumed, regardless of when the rest of the meal was eaten. At no time may meat and milk be eaten during the same meal, even though there may have been a sufficient time between meat and dairy.

For individuals whose health requires increased dairy intake, a one-hour period (or, in more severe cases, a lesser time period) may be permitted under guidance of competent authorities.

Foods that were prepared with meat, such as soups, broths and stews, etc., require the same waiting period, even though one did not consume the actual meat. When the foods were prepared without meat, but were merely cooked in clean meat pots, no waiting period is required. However, these foods should not intentionally be mixed directly with dairy foods or vice versa. If the foods were mixed inadvertently, a competent authority should be consulted.

After eating dairy foods, no waiting period is necessary, and it is sufficient to rinse the mouth and hands; with the

* The laws of this section are discussed in *Yoreh Deah* 89.

exception that after eating cheese which has been aged for six months or longer, the traditional six-hour time period is required before eating meat. (Since the age of the cheese is not always disclosed on the package, a competent authority should be consulted.)

☙ Housekeeping

Utensils*

Since meat and milk may not be mixed together, the preparation of dairy foods in pots that were used to prepare meat, or vice versa, is considered a meat and milk mixture. This is because when a utensil is used to heat food the pores of the container retain the flavor particles of the food substance and will release it when heated again. Thus if dairy food is cooked in a meat pot, the heated pot will release the meat flavor particles into the dairy food. This principle is the underlying reason for the traditional practice of keeping separate dishes, pots, pans, etc., for meat and dairy foods and the prohibition of using non-kosher utensils for kosher foods.

As a practical implementation of this principle, the observant kosher home maintains a full separation of all meat and milk utensils, with each readily identifiable. This avoids the possibility of using one to prepare food for the other. The maintenance of a kosher home or kitchen facility requires that a separate storage area be set aside for meat and dairy utensils, including pots, pans, dishes and flatware. If it is not feasible to assign separate cabinets, the shelves and drawers should be clearly designated for each type of utensil. Furthermore, the meat and dairy utensils

---

* The laws of this section are discussed in *Yoreh Deah* 93.

should be of substantially different color and design, to facilitate immediate identification and to avoid confusion. All members of the household should be made thoroughly familiar with the proper storage locations, and the distinct designs and colors of the separate sets.

In some instances it may be practical to maintain a set of *pareve* pots and pans, in which vegetables and other foods can be cooked and later used for either type of food. These too should be distinct in design or marked, so that they do not become mixed with the others. *Pareve* is the term used to describe foods of a neutral nature, neither milk nor meat. Interestingly enough, the origins of the word *pareve* are obscure, and it does not appear in the Torah, Talmud, or the Codes as a description of a category of food.

Glassware*

The status of glassware is a matter of Rabbinic discussion and tradition. Sephardic tradition maintains that since glassware does not retain the flavor particles of the foods itself it may be used interchangeably, while authorities of European origin (Ashkenazim) are of the opinion that since glass is earthenware in origin it may not be used interchangeably. This tradition is adhered to by the descendants of the European-Jewish communities. However, an exception is commonly made in the case of drinking glasses, since these are not used for heating foods. Once thoroughly washed they may be used for either variety.

Corelle, Pyrex, and glassware used for cooking must, of course, be kept separate.

* The laws of this section are discussed in *Orach Chaim* 451.

Milk and Meat at One Table*

Many times in home, school, or office dining rooms, people sit down to eat, each with his own food; some with dairy, some with meat; without realizing that they may not do so until precautions are taken to prevent the mixing and sharing of the foods. In order to prevent this possibility the Talmud requires that when people share the same table and eat meat and dairy foods they must either eat on separate tablecloths, or place some object on the table between them, to serve as a "dividing reminder" that the foods may not be shared or mixed. For this "reminder," one may use a candelabrum or even a whole loaf of bread that is not being eaten at that meal.

Authorities point out that when one eats alone, such a separation is not sufficient. Only one type of food — meat or dairy — should be on the table, unless another person is present to make sure that the foods are kept separate.

Condiments and Leftovers*

After a meat meal, the bread and the neutral (*pareve*) foods left over should not be used with meat, and vice versa. It is assumed that during the meal, either by handling or splattering, all these neutral foods came into contact with the foods being served and have a residue of meat or dairy on them. Exceptions of this rule are foods such as whole fruits and vegetables, which can be rinsed free of any residue. For this reason it is necessary to have separate meat and dairy dispensers for dressings, salt, pepper, sugar, mustards, jams, jellies, and other condiments. Here too it must be assumed that since they are left open on the table they either come in contact with the food or that some of the cutlery was used both for the foods and the condiments.

---

* The laws of this section are discussed in *Yoreh Deah* 88.

Table Linen*

Table linens and towels retain some of the food particles that they have been in contact with. However once they are thoroughly cleaned they may be used for any type of food.

Organization

It is obvious that the requirement to separate milk and meat in the kosher kitchen is a demanding one. At all times the kosher kitchen must be well organized and tidy. For example, leftover meat or dairy dishes or pots improperly stored can easily render other foods and utensils unfit. The failure to prevent cluttering is most likely to cause meat and dairy to become mistakenly mixed. It is essential to recognize that organization is the key in establishing the kitchen procedures necessary to maintain kashruth requirements.

Equally necessary is the need to maintain orderly cleaning and washing systems in the kitchen. It is not difficult to visualize what could happen if dirty dishes are left from one meal to the next. The sink and countertops would then become areas of confusion, and proper kashruth could not be truly observed. Obviously, the only practical solution is that the cleaning and storage of all meat and dairy dishes should be prompt and orderly.

After the dishes have been washed, the sink itself should be washed clean. Once washed, the sink may be used for either meat or dairy, provided the dishes are placed on a strainer rack. Of course, different racks should be used for meat and dairy.

If the dishes are to be soaked, individual soaking pans for meat and dairy should be used.

---

* The laws of this section are discussed in *Yoreh Deah* 88.

Fish*

The Torah (*Leviticus* 11:9 and 10) describes the permitted species of fish and marine life: "This is what you may eat in the water, whatever has fins and scales."

Once it has been determined that a fish has scales, it may be assumed that it has fins as well and that the fish is kosher. The Talmud cites the natural phenomenon that all fish that have kosher scales have fins. The converse is not true, however; the presence of fins is not an indication that there are scales.

"Scales" are defined as ones that can be scraped from the skin without tearing the skin from the flesh. These are cycloid (round) and ctenoid (comblike) scales. Other types of scales such as placoid and ganoid (platelike, armorlike) are embedded in the skin, and it is necessary to remove some of

* The laws of this section are discussed in *Yoreh Deah* 83, 116.

the skin or flesh in order to remove them. Bony tubercules that protrude from the skin are not considered scales, and fishes with such structures are non-kosher. The lumpfish, sturgeon, sharks, swordfish, and some of the turbots (European flatfish) are examples of fishes with types of scales that are not of the kosher variety. Catfishes, monkfish and sculpins are examples of fishes without any scales. Since crustaceans and mollusks (shellfish) have no scales, they too are non-kosher, as are the marine mammals: seals, dolphins, porpoises and whales.

It is advisable for kashruth observers to become familiar with the kosher type of scale. This can be learned by simply examining the various kinds of kosher fishes and observing their scales. Although this does not make one an expert, it nevertheless does provide the experience needed to recognize fishes that are questionable. When a question does arise, the guidance of experts should be sought.

The common names used for fish are not always an accurate means of identification. They, too, can be misleading, since these names may vary in different parts of the country. The colloquial name used to describe a fish in one place may be used for another, different kind of fish somewhere else. The only absolutely reliable name is the unique scientific Latin one given by scientists to each species of the fish.*

The Torah description of permissible fish with fins and scales includes species that do not develop their scales until the later stages of their lives, as well as those that have scales and later lose them, e.g., sardines which may be caught and processed when they are immature and have not yet developed scales, and certain kinds of herrings which shed their scales when they are taken from the water.

A fish is kosher regardless of the number and size of the scales on its body. However, a species of fish that develops

---

*A listing of the names of properly-scaled and non-kosher fish is provided as an appendix to this volume.

only one scale must have this scale located near the jaw, fin -or tail, but if it develops more than one scale, they may be located anywhere on the body in order to be kosher. Fishes that have very thin and minute scales require expert examination in order to determine whether their scales are of the kosher variety.

When the skin of a fish has been removed, the filleted flesh is no longer identifiable as kosher. Filleted fish, whether fresh, canned, frozen, ground or sliced, should not be accepted unless the kosher origin of the fish is guaranteed. A label declaration stating the species of the fish is inadequate to guarantee the kosher origin of the fish sold with the skin removed. In addition to the kashruth control necessary for the filleting of fish, other production processes, as well, must be kashruth guaranteed, including all methods of curing, smoking, and pickling. The curing and smoking processes of fish are often done in plants where non-kosher fish are cured and smoked. Full kashruth control is necessary to insure that kosher fishes are not processed with non-kosher ones.

Pickled fish products must be kashruth guaranteed to insure the origin of the fish, the production procedures, and the ingredients used. Kashruth control guarantees that the vinegar is of kosher origin, and is neither non-kosher wine vinegar nor the product of a vinegar produced from wine alcohol. The spices used in the preparation of such popular pickled fish as herring are prepared with specialty blends and additives which may contain glycerides to aid in the solubility of the spice. Some herring products include wine in the recipe, and these too must be kashruth guaranteed.

The market where one purchases fresh fish requires careful scrutiny to insure that the fishes are not cut on the same boards and with the same knives that are used for non-kosher species. The precautions and restrictions for filleted fish at a retail outlet are the same as those for commercial producers, and the fish should be filleted either in front of the consumer or another observant Jew, or a part of the skin should be left on each slice so that the scales can be seen.

Fish are a *pareve* (neutral) food. The entire fish, including the blood, may be eaten and requires no special preparation. Since fish are neither meat nor dairy, they may be eaten before and after any food. However, Talmudic tradition prohibits the eating of any mixtures of meat and fish, and requires rinsing one's mouth after eating one before eating the other. Many authorities maintain that the restriction is limited to eating the foods together. Utensils used to cook the foods, once thoroughly washed and clean, may be used interchangeably for either food, provided they are not cooked together. Other authorities maintain that the utensils should be kept separate. However, there are no restrictions for the interchange of table cutlery and dinnerware, which may be used for either meat and fish, after being washed clean.

Eggs*

Many of us are probably familiar from early childhood with the scene of a mother or grandmother cracking eggs, dropping them into a glass, and examining them for blood spots. This practice is so traditional that we may not fully understand its origin.

A blood spot on a fertilized egg is a sign of the possible beginning of the formation of a chicken embryo, and therefore both the blood and the entire egg are forbidden. Among the Talmudic commentators there are several opinions as to exactly where on the egg a blood spot is indicative of germ development. Based on these discussions, and the fact that it is often difficult to determine the precise area on the egg where the blood does not indicate development of an embryo, it is traditional kashruth

* The laws of this section are discussed in *Yoreh Deah* 66.

practice to discard all eggs found to have blood spots.

Often the spot is found after the egg has been mixed with other eggs. In these cases, when the mixture consists of the spotted egg and two or more additional eggs, there are diverse opinions. Some authorities maintain that when the spot is located on the yolk, all the eggs must be discarded. However, when the location of the spot cannot be determined or it is found on the albumen (i.e., the white), the mixture is permitted, and only the spot and as much of the egg as possible need be removed.

Other authorities rule that only the spot and as much as possible of the egg need be discarded, regardless of whether the spot was found on the yolk or the albumen. In each instance, should the question arise, expert guidance should be sought. The authorities must also be consulted when a spotted egg is found to have been mixed with other foods.

Kashruth observers often ask: "Is it necessary to examine each egg for a blood spot; and what of eggs that have not been examined?" Eggs that have not been examined are permissible; since the large majority of eggs are free of blood spots, we may assume that the eggs are part of that natural majority, and their kashruth is not in question. Nevertheless, in order to avoid complications should a spot be found, it is the universal kashruth practice to examine each egg individually before use.

Since the prohibition of blood spots is based on the possibility that the blood is that of an embryo germ, the eggs of hens that have been completely isolated and inaccessible to roosters are permitted, since such eggs cannot possibly be fertilized. In this type of egg only the spot need be removed, and the rest of the egg is kosher.

However, since blood spots themselves are an indication that an egg may have been fertile, it is necessary to establish the fact of the absolute isolation of the hens. In the United States where flocks of laying hens are housed in large fully automated and controlled-environment coops, it is very rare for roosters to be present in the same area as the hens, and therefore there is little possibility that the egg is fertile. Nevertheless, authorities maintain that the practice of discarding the individual spotted egg should be adhered to. However, a more lenient view may be followed when these eggs have been mixed with other eggs; the mixture is permissible and only the blood spot itself need be removed. Nor is the kashruth of the pots used for cooking such eggs affected if the eggs are found to be spotted.

Many food outlets selling natural and health foods also include "natural eggs" from hens that are not maintained in controlled environments, and are free roaming. The eggs of these hens are, of course, assumed to be fertilized and the blood-spotted eggs are forbidden.

(Frozen and powdered eggs are discussed on pages 65-67.)

Dairy

◆§ Chaleiv Yisrael (Supervised Milk)*

The restriction is stated in the Talmud that milk produced without the presence of an observant Jew at the milking may not be consumed. This restriction prevents the possibility of the mixing of the milk of non-kosher animals with the milk of kosher animals.

It is a matter of halachic discussion and responsa whether the situation in the United States — where government agriculture and health authorities maintain control over milk production, and the adulteration of milk is a punishable offense — may be regarded as equal to the surveillance required by the Talmud. Many maintain that

* The laws of this section are discussed in *Yoreh Deah* 115.

these controls are sufficient. Others maintain that the requirement of the Talmud can be met only by the personal presence and supervision of an observant Jew. To meet the needs of the adherents of this view, *chaleiv Yisrael,* supervised milk, is produced.

For many years kosher supervision of milk, other than for Passover, was hardly known in the United States. It is true that there were a few scattered pious Jews who either drank no milk or made their own arrangements to supervise milk at a nearby dairy. At that time the majority of kashruth observers throughout the United States consumed the milk produced by commercial dairies.

It would be incorrect to state that during this pre-World War II period *chaleiv Yisrael* [i.e., milk produced under Jewish supervision] was "unheard of." Throughout the entire European Jewish religious community and the Mediterranean, North African and Asian Sephardic *kehillos* the restriction was meticulously observed. With the influx of large numbers of observant Jews into the New York area just prior to the outbreak of World War II, there became a growing awareness and a subsequent demand for kosher-supervised milk. The demand was substantial enough for two small local dairies located within the New York City limits to produce enough supervised milk to satisfy the needs of the religious community.

Slowly the numbers of *chaleiv Yisrael* users grew. With the passage of time more communities have established supervision at dairy facilities, not only in the New York City area. In metropolitan centers throughout the United States *chaleiv Yisrael* is now available in many retail outlets, and is no longer an obscure kashruth technicality.

Those who accept the view that government controls are sufficient must bear in mind that this is relevant only in the United States, or in other countries wherein the effect of the governmental control is similar. However, in parts of the world where there is no concern on the part of the authorities, or where the governments are weak and/or corrupted, the milk generally produced is not permitted, and *chaleiv Yisrael* is required. In addition, in some Eastern European countries, especially in the Balkans, and in Asia and Africa, it is common for farmers to milk their mares and camels. A popular sour dairy food in these areas – koumiss – is produced from mare's milk. In these countries, also, the restriction is in full effect.

Unfortunately many American travelers are unaware that in many areas *chaleiv Yisrael* is a kashruth requirement, and that the opinions followed in the United States permitting consumption of general-production milk are not universally applicable.

◆§ Cheese*

Cheese is the subject of Talmudic restriction, in addition to all other kashruth requirements. The prohibition is referred to as *g'vinas akum* (cheese produced by a non-Jew).

The prohibition of *g'vinas akum* is a result of the method by which cheese is manufactured. Cheese is produced naturally by coagulating milk. This coagulation is caused by the addition to milk of the mucosa found in the stomach linings of calves. Where cheese is produced by non-Jews there is an assumption that the stomach linings used were non-kosher, and the cheese is therefore forbidden. The prohibition described in the *Mishnah* regarding *g'vinas akum* includes all cheese manufactured by non-Jews, even if all the ingredients of the cheese are kosher. Only cheese of Jewish production, or overseen by observant Jews, is permissible, provided the rennin coagulant used is kosher-produced from the linings of kosher-slaughtered, properly

* The laws of this section are discussed in *Yoreh Deah* 115.

prepared and dried calf stomachs. Included in this restriction are all hard cheeses, e.g., Swiss, Cheddar, Muenster, Mozzarella, Gouda, Colby, Salud, etc.

This method of production is similar to cheese production in modern times; however, instead of using the stomach lining itself to coagulate the milk, extracts of the lining which contain the rennin enzyme are processed, and used in cheese and other dairy products. The forbidden extract containing the rennin enzyme is called rennet, and is described below in the additive section under "Rennin." Rennet substitutes have been developed by microbial means, and milk-clotting enzymes for cheese making are produced from fungi. These microbial enzymes are sometimes referred to as "microbial rennet," though rennet is a technical term used solely for the enzyme derived from the stomach linings of calves.

The status of cottage cheese, ricotta, and similar soft cheeses is a matter of Talmudic discussion. Some maintain that the restriction applies to all cheeses, both soft and hard. Others maintain that such soft cheeses as cottage cheese when produced with kosher ingredients are permissible, and may be regarded as similar to other cultured dairy products, e.g., sour cream, yogurt, buttermilk, etc., and are not subject to the prohibition of *g'vinas akum.*

These cultured dairy products also require careful kashruth scrutiny, and should not be mistakenly assumed to be kosher simply because they are dairy, for they may contain non-kosher additives. In many parts of the United States gelatin is added to yogurt and to its fruit contents. Swiss-style yogurts (smooth yogurts), sour cream or buttermilk are often produced with rennet and glycerides. Some dairies add glycerides to sweet cream in order to improve the mixing qualities of the product. (See additive section: GELATIN; GLYCERIDES; RENNIN; and WHEY.)

Butter and Margarine*

Butter is not included in the milk or cheese restrictions of non-Jewish dairy products. This is because butter is not a cheese product, and because the Talmud states that the milk of a non-kosher animal does not coagulate, and therefore cannot be churned into butter. As a result, many of those who strictly adhere to the restriction requiring supervised milk do not require that butter be made from that type of milk. Other authorities, however, maintain the custom requiring butter to be produced from supervised milk.

During the existence of the Jewish communities of Eastern Europe, Jews refrained from the use of non-Jewish butter, since there was the suspicion that the butter was adulterated with non-kosher fats. The same was true in some Eastern countries, where there was suspicion that means were developed of producing butter with a blend of camels' milk. Today as well, in many areas outside the United States there exists the possibility of adulteration in the production of butter.

In the United States, in addition to cream, butter is produced with culture starters and annato or carotene coloring. (See FOOD-COLORING and BETA-CAROTENE in additive section.) Some manufacturers have begun producing a butter-oleomargarine blend, and label their product accordingly. Oleomargarine is produced from oils and fats together with glycerides, artificial butter flavor and color. It is packaged and marketed as a substitute for butter, and has gained popularity since it has the advantage of being low in cholesterol and saturated fats. Margarines may be produced either with or without milk, and should not be assumed to be *pareve* unless so designated. Since margarine is produced

* The laws of this section are discussed in *Yoreh Deah* 115.

with glycerides, oils, fats and flavoring, it and all products containing margarine must be effectively kashruth guaranteed. (See additive section: GLYCERIDES; HYDROGENATED SHORTENING; FLAVORINGS.)

☙ Ice Cream

Ice cream is one of the most popular dairy products, and contrary to the popular misconception, the practice of kashruth control is essential. In its simplest form ice cream can be produced from a formula consisting of cream, milk, sugar and/or corn syrup, and the basic flavorings of cocoa, coffee, and vanilla. However, the commercial production of such a formula on a mass scale is not economically viable.

Manufacturers of ice cream must develop a product that is smooth in texture and full flavored, and with the long freezer life and slow-melt qualities that make ice cream so pleasurable. In order to accomplish this, a complete range of stabilizers, glyceride emulsifiers, vegetable gums, and alginates are added. Each of these products is fully described in our additive section.

Many producers find it more efficient to purchase ready-mixed blends of ice cream stabilizers which contain all the necessary gums, emulsifiers and alginates for ice cream production. Some of these blends contain added milk proteins and whey, a cheese by-product described in the additive section. The structure of these blends makes it possible for the manufacturer to reduce the amount of cream in his product, thus reducing his cost significantly, and still maintain a quality standard.

Ice cream/stabilizer blends are multipurpose and are produced in a variety of formulations for use in the full range of frozen dessert products, e.g., soft ice creams, frozen yogurts, custards. These types of stabilizer formulations are also used in non-dairy and imitation ice cream foods, since these too require the texture and "mouthfeel" qualities of ice cream.

Ice cream blends and mixes are also the base for ice cream produced in franchised retail outlets, which are equipped with machinery to produce the ice cream sold in the store. Each of these facilities must, therefore, be regarded as an individual factory, and the production in the store must be effectively controlled if the kashruth is to be guaranteed. It is incorrect to assume that since one or more stores of a franchise are kosher-endorsed the entire chain may be accepted as kosher. Each franchisee operates and produces his own product; kashruth control is therefore necessary, since the individual store is an independent ice cream producer. This rule holds true in every franchise-type food operation, where the acceptability of one should not be assumed as a guarantee of any other.

In addition to the stabilizers and mixed blends which give the product its body and texture, there are the flavorings which furnish the pleasant taste sensations of ice cream. These flavors must be specially prepared for use in ice cream products, since they blend evenly in milkfat and have the ability to counteract the "off flavors" of the emulsifying additives, the milk, cream and whey, and remain stable under freezing temperatures.

In the additive section on flavors, both natural and artificial, we describe in detail the need for kashruth guarantees on flavorings and full control of this critical product. In addition to these basic ingredients, ice creams may contain a variety of coatings, candies, cake, cookies, toppings and fruit fillings. Each of these products is purchased ready made by the producer. These products too must be kashruth controlled, since they are manufactured with fats, oils, emulsifiers, eggs, flavors and stabilizers.

It is obvious that ice cream is a critical food product, which should not be accepted as kosher unless the entire manufacturing procedure and all ingredients are under effective kashruth control.

Bakery Products

◆§ Bread, Rolls, Challa*

This household staple has long been the subject of misconceptions regarding the need for kashruth caution before accepting it into the home. Some have assumed that while pastries and other specialty bakery items require kashruth guarantees, basic bread items, especially the popular ethnic varieties of rye and pumpernickel, need not be questioned. This practice has led to the belief that bread, bagels and even *challa* may be obtained from sources where the pastry items are not acceptable. A revived kashruth sophistication has encouraged the abandonment of these

* The laws of this section are discussed in *Yoreh Deah* 97.

misconceptions. As a result of increased public demand in many communities, locally produced bread and baked goods are effectively kashruth controlled.

It is of course true that in its simplest form bread may be produced from flour, water, yeast and salt. However, bread production on a commercial basis demands a more complicated formula to insure quality standards of flavor, texture and shelf life. Without proper kashruth guidance even the well-intentioned baker may by error use non-kosher ingredients in the product.

The need to insure a consistently high quality of dough has compelled manufacturers to enhance the process of dough production. Dough conditioners, softeners and specialty shortenings are vital in the preparation of a bread that will maintain freshness long after its homemade counterpart has gone stale. In addition many bakers, to improve and standardize their formulae, make their product with specially formulated bread mixes, which are available for each type of bread, e.g., white, whole wheat, rye, pumpernickel, French, Italian, *challa,* health breads, etc. These products contain all the necessary fats, oils, glycerides, stabilizers, flavorings and other additives in precise proportions. Unless these products are effectively kashruth guaranteed, they must be assumed to be non-kosher.

The question of kashruth of bread is not limited to the ingredient content of the dough. After the batters are mixed the prepared dough is placed in a trough, vat or pan and allowed to rise. These vessels are greased with an oil-based release agent, which prevents the dough from sticking to the surface. Release agents are produced from mineral oil, vegetable fats and oils, animal tallow, or a blend of any of these. Unless the source and manufacturing process of these release agents are kashruth controlled, they may not be used in kosher production.

All other foods to which milk and dairy products have been added merely become dairy foods, and are to be eaten only with other dairy, or *pareve* foods. Unique to bread is the Talmudic law which requires that all dough used in preparing bread be *pareve,* containing neither meat nor dairy. This is because bread is considered the staple of the diet, and is eaten with all types of meals. Only by completely restricting the use of dairy or meat breads in Jewish homes is the possibility of eating the bread with the improper meal eliminated.

When the bread is baked in a unique form that identifies it as different, or when it is baked in individual portions, enough only for one person at one meal, the addition of milk or meat is permitted. The identification of the bread, or its being in individual portions, is effective only when it is so at the time of baking. If the bread is identified afterwards, or sliced into individual portions, it is nevertheless restricted, since at the time of baking there was no identification or portioning.

Many bakers consider milk, milk powder, whey and casein (milk proteins) as vital ingredients in their products, adding strength and texture to the dough. These producers insist that there is no substitute for the quality of milk. The ingredient list of most commercially produced baked items gives evidence to this fact. Many retail bakers are reluctant to produce baked items without this vital ingredient for fear that the finished product will not meet their personal quality standards. It is not uncommon for otherwise decent individuals to be overcome with a desire to make a truly good product and succumb to the temptation of adding milk to their pastries, buns, bread and *challa.* Experience teaches that the presence of milk and milk products in a commercial bakery presents a danger of temptation for misuse in *pareve* products, and their designation for use in specific varieties of pastries is insufficient unless stringent methods for effective control are in force.

Bagels

Similar to the misconceptions regarding bread are those related to bagels, which many consumers assume to be free of additives and universally kosher. Many bagel outlets produce their product from especially formulated bagel mixes which contain a variety of dough conditioners and specialty ingredients of possible non-kosher origin. In addition bagel doughs, too, require the use of release agents, and the source of all of these materials must be kashruth controlled.

(See the chapter "Pas Akum and Bishul Akum" for further discussion about baked goods.)

◆§ Cakes and Pastries

Production of cakes and pastries incorporates not only the need for all the kashruth vigilance required for bread, but adds its own requirements. Cakes and pastries are produced from many specialty ingredients, each designed for a specific purpose in the cake recipe. Such common pastries as Danish, strudel and pie dough are produced with specialty shortening blends. These fats are added to the batter in order to help produce the unique textures. In the general market many of these types of shortenings are produced from a blend of lard and vegetable oils, since the chemical composition of animal fats is ideal for the production of pie crust, strudel dough and Danish pastries. The kosher baker must find suitable kashruth guaranteed vegetable-source shortenings for his pastry needs, often at a premium in price.

Critical too in pastry production is the adequate supply of whole eggs, yolks and egg whites. Nearly every bakery recipe calls for the use of some type of egg or egg-based product, either as an ingredient in the product or as a coating to provide the baked goods with a sheen.

To the average consumer the use of eggs creates concern for elimination of blood-spotted eggs. However, most commercial bakers find it impractical to store, crack and separate eggs. Therefore they purchase eggs that have already been shelled and processed, either frozen or powdered – yolks, whites and whole eggs. The source of supply of these processed eggs is critical to a kosher operation.

In the United States all egg processors engaged in interstate commerce must be approved by the Department of Agriculture, which carries out an inspection of all plants. Under present regulations these plants may process the eggs of both live and slaughtered hens. The eggs removed from the slaughtered hen are referred to as ova and are non-kosher. In many poultry slaughterhouses, eggs are removed during evisceration and sold in bulk to processors, who in turn separate and pasteurize the ova for sale to bakers and other food producers. Present government regulations recognize ova as a wholesome food and indistinguishable from the eggs of live hens except in name. The regulations only require that the eggs of slaughtered hens be identified as ova, and not referred to as eggs. Since ova is a natural by-product of slaughtered hens, it is sold at a price lower than the eggs of live hens, and is available through commercial outlets.

Many egg processors have found it to their advantage to produce both ova and eggs. This practice creates a critical kashruth situation. All processed eggs must be pasteurized. The eggs of live hens are often pasteurized together with ova and thus become non-kosher. Proper kashruth control of a bakery and other food producers using eggs makes it necessary to guarantee not only the elimination of ova, but that the manufacturing procedure of the eggs of live hens must be authentically kashruth controlled and guaranteed.

The use of commercially processed eggs is further

complicated when the products of foreign producers are used. It is often difficult to determine the processing procedures in force abroad for ova production, and therefore these products should be avoided.

Federal government regulations also permit eggs processed in Oriental countries, where some of the species of egg-producing hens are not known by tradition to be of kosher origin.

It is evident to the knowledgeable kashruth observer that the misguided perception that there is "nothing wrong with a Danish or a piece of pie" is a misconception and that baked goods require scrutiny and kashruth control.

In addition to these products, no bakery is complete without a full line of flavorings, fillings, frostings and toppings; each of which must be kashruth guaranteed. The additive section of this book describes in detail the need for kashruth control of flavors.

Kashruth control is necessary in the production of toppings, frostings and fillings in order to eliminate the use of gelatin as a stabilizing base, and to insure that the fats, oils, glyceride emulsifiers, flavorings and eggs that are commonly used in these products are of kosher origin.

Fruit fillings, too, contain additives necessary to provide product consistency. These fillings are specially produced with a variety of stabilizers that prevent running and leaking under the heat of baking, and each of the raw materials used must be kashruth guaranteed.

Pas Akum and Bishul Akum

◆ Foods Produced by Non-Jews*

As a deterrent against assimilation and intermarriage, restrictions were established that maintain the distinction of the Jewish home and faith. The *Mishnah* enumerates the prohibitions of:

(1) *pas akum* or *pas nochri* — bread and baked goods baked by non-Jews;
(2) *bishul akum* (foods cooked by non-Jews);
(3) *yayin nesech* (the wine of non-Jews).

* The laws of this section are discussed in *Yoreh Deah* 112, 113.

☙§ Pas Palter (Commercial Bread)

Many authorities maintain that the restriction of non-Jewish baked bread is distinct from the other restrictions, and limits only breads that are home-baked for personal use. However, non-Jewish bread that is commercially baked [*pas palter*] is excluded from the prohibition, and it is common practice, therefore, to accept kosher-approved bread produced by commercial bakeries.

Others maintain that the commercial bread is permitted only when it is either the only source or the best product available. Still others make no distinction between commercial and non-commercial breads, and restrict both. When both types are available of equal quality, full observance of the restriction is preferable.

Many authorities point out another unique exception to this prohibition, namely that a guest is permitted to eat commercial non-Jewish bread offered by a host in order to prevent any ill will that would arise from his refusal.

Non-Jewish baked goods become universally acceptable when simple steps are taken to assist in the baking. This is accomplished either by igniting or otherwise adding to the flame or heat source, i.e., stirring the coals, raising the fire, or adding even the smallest piece of wood to the fire. Once this has been done the product is permissible according to all authorities.

Baked cakes and cookies are considered similar to bread, and are permitted by those who permit commercial non-Jewish baked goods. However, this similarity to bread applies only to *stiff* batters, because, if they are eaten in sufficiently large quantities, the blessing *Hamotzi* and Grace After Meals are required. Consequently they are treated as bread. Fried or cooked *loose* batters, however, never require *Hamotzi* and full Grace After Meals, regardless of the quantity consumed; therefore they are not subject to the laws of bread. Instead they are subject to the laws of *bishul akum* (see below). If a loose batter is baked, however, it is treated as *pas akum*.

Bread and baked goods are only those products produced from the flour of the grains: wheat, rye, oats, spelt and barley. Baked goods produced from other flours are not considered bread, and the laws of *bishul akum* apply. Baked goods produced with a blend of both grain and other flours, i.e., rice, corn, etc., may still be considered bread, depending on the amount of grain in the blend. In these cases expert guidance should be sought.

☙ Bishul Akum (Foods Cooked by Non-Jews)

The prohibition of foods cooked by non-Jews, *bishul akum,* is more extensive than that of baked goods, and includes both foods prepared for personal use and commercial products. *Bishul akum* restricts foods that are prepared by cooking, roasting, frying, etc. However, foods that are prepared without heat by pickling and curing are permitted. Also excluded from this prohibition are foods that are prepared by smoking.

Bishul akum is limited to foods that cannot easily be eaten raw, and that are fit to be served at a royal table either as part of a meal or as a delicacy. Thus, the prohibition would not apply to many cooked fruits and vegetables, which can be eaten raw, or to such foods as cooked corn which is generally regarded as unfit for a royal repast. In order to establish precisely which foods are prohibited and which are permitted, it is necessary to review each category with competent authorities.

According to Ashkenazic tradition, it is not required that

a Jew do all the cooking; the ignition or addition to the heat source by a Jew is sufficient to permit foods to be cooked by non-Jews. Thus, once the flame is ignited by a Jew, non-Jews may cook with flames lit from it. This is especially helpful in homes and facilities with non-Jewish help, where care must be taken that the foods cooked should not be *bishul akum.*

In later years discussion arose regarding the status of foods prepared by steam. Some authorities consider this method of food preparation similar to smoked foods, and permissible, while others maintain that the food is to be considered "cooked" and is therefore prohibited.

Foods prepared in large factories, too, are the subject of responsa and differing views. Since commercially cooked foods are forbidden as are home/personally prepared foods, many authorities argue that the prohibition is all inclusive and that it applies as well to mass-produced industrial products. Others argue that a distinction may be made between the foods of a small commercial outlet, which are prohibited, and those prepared in large factories, where there can be no social contact between the many anonymous employees and the consumer. While many do not accept this view, they do point out that there is reason to permit foods prepared by steaming in these large factories. Since frozen fruits and vegetables require further cooking before they can be eaten, they are not considered *bishul akum,* even though they have been blanched.

Yayin nesech, non-Jewish wine, is discussed below in the following chapter.

Alcoholic Beverages

Distilled Beverages

Alcoholic beverages are unique among processed foods in that federal law at present does not require a listing of ingredients. The dedicated kashruth observer must, therefore, be able to recognize the problem areas of alcoholic beverages and mixers.

Whiskey

Of primary concern is the source of the alcohol itself: whether it is of grain, fruit or wine origin. Whiskeys (e.g., bourbon, rye, Scotch, Canadian) are produced from grain alcohol. Rum is produced from sugar alcohol. Most vodkas and gin are produced from grain alcohol, as indicated on the product label: "distilled from grain;" or "100% grain neutral spirits." Some are produced from other varieties of alcohol, and, in rare instances, from alcohol produced from milk by-products. Though whiskey may be produced with any additive permitted by government regulation, these ingredients are zealously guarded secrets of the individual distillers.

Brandy

Brandy and cognac are produced by the distillation of wine. The retrieved alcohol is aged in casks, where it mellows and develops its special flavor qualities. Cognac is a brandy that has been produced from the grapes of the Cognac region in France. Since the wine of these grapes produce a very fine brandy, the name cognac is used to describe the product.

Liqueur

A wide variety of flavored liqueurs, both of imported and domestic production, are available in the marketplace, and some of the popular international brands have unwittingly found their way into kosher homes. Many kashruth observers are not aware that these liqueurs may be either wine or wine-alcohol based, or are the product of fruit and fruit essences that have been steeped in brandy. The very popular almond-apricot liqueur known as amaretto is made in this fashion. Therefore, it is essential to bear in mind that liqueurs and brandies may not be used unless their kashruth is guaranteed.

In addition to the alcohol base, scrutiny must be given to the flavors added to liqueurs. These require effective kashruth control in order to guarantee the source of the flavor ingredients.

Some alcoholic beverages are sold as preblended cream liqueurs. These liqueurs are produced with glycerides, and other fats and emulsifiers of non-kosher origin.

Drink mixers, too, may contain non-kosher ingredients (i.e., vermouth wine, foaming and creaming agents, and flavors). These products, therefore, require authentic kashruth guarantees.

The type of alcohol used in the production of specific alcoholic products may be based on specific unchanging formulae or upon prevailing market conditions, in which case the consumer cannot be sure of the contents. It is common that when wines are of inferior quality, or in times of oversupply, wine is distilled, and the alcohol produced is sold at lower prices. Since the type of alcohol used in liqueur production may vary based upon prevailing market conditions, a manufacturer's claim as to the nature of the ingredients should not by itself be accepted as an adequate kashruth guarantee.

(See additive section: ETHANOL; GLYCERIDES.)

Social Drinking

The common practice of social drinking presents a challenge to the maintenance of kashruth standards in business and social situations. In addition to questions of the kashruth of the ingredients, however, it is vital for kashruth observers to recognize that at all times alcohol consumption must be kept at the disciplined levels that do not compromise Torah standards of ethical conduct and self-discipline.

Wine

Non-Jewish Production

Wine must be produced under special handling procedures based on the Torah which forbids the use, consumption or any other benefit from wine that has been used as a libation in a pagan religious rite. This restriction is described in the familiar term of *yayin nesech,* wine poured for a libation (*Deuteronomy* 32:38).

The prohibition forbidding wine used in a pagan rite was extended to forbid consumption and any use or benefit from any wine produced by non-Jews, regardless of whether or not they were wines of libation. The establishment of the prohibition is explained in the Talmud as a means to eliminate the possibility of use of pagan libations, and to prevent Jewish intermarriage and assimilation with followers of other faiths. The extended prohibition includes wine that was produced or handled by non-Jews.

The scholars of the Gaonic period limited the prohibition of use or benefit to wines of polytheistic non-Jews who worship pagan deities. The wines of monotheistic non-Jews are restricted only for consumption, and their use or benefit is permitted. Others maintain that the permission of use or benefit may be extended even to those of polytheistic faiths, as long as they do not practice the religious rite of wine libation.

The wine prohibitions also include Jews committed to heresy and denial of the Jewish faith.

Both the fresh juice of grapes and the fermented wines of non-Jews are forbidden. Wines produced from the juices of other fruits are permitted. Non-kosher grape juices and wines that have been further fermented, distilled and

---

* The laws of this section are discussed in *Yoreh Deah* 123, 124, 132, 134.

processed to produce vinegar, alcohol, brandy, cognac, jellies, jam and other food items are not kosher, since they are the product of non-kosher juice and wine.

The Talmud describes the handling of wine by non-Jews [*maga akum*] as wine that has been both touched and stroked intentionally, either directly by hand or indirectly with a tool or other hand-held implement. The same is true of an open container of wine that has been lifted and shaken.

Since the wine prohibition is based on the Torah declaration forbidding wine of pagan religious rites, the prohibition is applied only to wines commonly used for that purpose. This excludes kosher wines that have been cooked. The cooking of a wine [*yayin mevushal*] depletes its full quality and flavor, and though the product is still considered wine, it may be handled by anyone once it has been cooked. There are various opinions as to the level of heat to which a juice or wine must be subjected for it to be considered "cooked." Many authorities maintain that once heated to a temperature of approximately 170°F the wine is considered cooked. Other authorities require a higher temperature. Kosher wines and grape juices that are to be served and handled by non-Jews in kashruth-guaranteed facilities must be pre-cooked.

The pasteurization of juices and wines are the subject of many responsa. Many authorities maintain that the pasteurization process constitutes cooking, and wines produced from pasteurized juices are under no handling restrictions. Other authorities argue that since flash pasteurization is a process by which the wine is heated for a few seconds and then chilled in a closed unit, it has a negligible affect on the juice or wine and does not render it *yayin mevushal.*

Fruit wines and brandies may be produced from fermented fruit juices other than grape. However, the consumer should not assume that a product is kosher merely because a specific fruit is identified on the label. Many of these beverages are blends of fruit concentrates with non-kosher vermouth wine, while others are produced by blending either the fruits or fruit alcohol with wine alcohol. These types of beverages may not be used unless their kashruth has been authentically established and guaranteed.

By-products

Distilled wine products produced from kosher wines, e.g., alcohol, brandy and cognac, may be handled by anyone since distillation is a cooking process. Vinegar produced from kosher wine may also be handled by anyone, since alcohol that has completely fermented into acetic acid (vinegar) is no longer considered wine.

Neither are there any restrictions as to handling a wine that has been completely diluted. If the wine content is less than a sixth of the mixture, it is considered diluted.

Additives

The kosher status of wine is determined by the additives used to control the natural fermentation process, and by the method of production and the special handling that are required in order for the wine to be fully kashruth controlled.

There are over sixty additives that winemakers may use in the production of wine. Among them are sulfites, sugar and/or corn syrup, nutrients, stabilizers, clarifiers, smoothing agents, acidifiers, acid reducers, enzymes and alcohol to improve the quality of the wine. Since each step of the wine-making process demands special handling and kashruth control, the nature of the wine-ingredient additives are critical to the control system. (See additive section: ENZYMES; SULFITES.)

The Kosher Traveler

Being away from home places the kosher traveler in a situation where the need for kashruth acumen and ingenuity is critical. Unless properly prepared for the challenge, the kosher traveler is often tempted to compromise and temporarily accept whatever kosher facilities are available, setting aside the kashruth standards to which he adheres at home. Experience has taught the kosher traveler that a practice of poor food selection soon leads to physical difficulties and compromised kashruth discipline. Both can result from attempting to survive on one small meal a day, while replacing real food with snacks of coffee, candy and cake. It is essential to bear in mind that it is possible to be satisfactorily nourished on the road and still maintain honest kashruth requirements without great difficulty. This is accomplished when the traveler takes the time to plan ahead and develop the know-how to improvise in order to provide basic kashruth needs.

When traveling in the United States, the problems are fewer due to the ready availability of supermarkets and service-oriented hotels. The first task for the traveler is to learn whether there are kosher facilities, and how convenient they are to his place of business or hotel. Unfortunately travelers are misled by the idea that their problems are solved because they have learned of a kosher luncheonette, restaurant or pizza store in the city, without realizing that the travel time to and from their location may prove too disruptive for the purposes of the trip. It is also necessary to determine whether the hours and types of food served are suitable for the needs of the traveler.

Careful research must be done to determine the level of kashruth integrity of the facilities that are to be patronized. This task is often the most difficult to accomplish at long distance. For a variety of reasons, knowledgeable people are often hesitant to give negative responses and clear-cut answers. A kosher traveler must be firmly committed to the principle that a facility must earn his full confidence before it will be patronized. Kashruth observance is an essential act of Torah faith. Truly dedicated religious Jews must be conditioned to live up to their ideals wherever they may find themselves.

Not only should the scrupulous kosher traveler fully maintain kashruth discipline while away from home, but it is an absolute necessity that he assure himself of the hygienic conditions of the food preparation. Experienced travelers can well document the danger and terror of compromise in hygiene. Nothing can be more demoralizing to kashruth discipline.

The next problem facing the traveler is the ability to be self-sufficient when there are no adequate facilities. This condition is not always as difficult as it may appear at first.

With time, planning and a willingness to improvise, a variety of satisfactory meals can be prepared. The key to self-sufficiency is the ability to purchase and store small amounts of food. It is essential that the traveler locate a conveniently located supermarket where the necessary foods and supplies can be obtained.

The second step is to provide for storage of the food. Some hotels and motels will provide a small portable refrigerator. This is ideal for the kosher traveler. When this is not available a makeshift ice chest can be improvised by lining the waste basket with plastic bags and filling them with ice cubes. Some travelers find it convenient to purchase inexpensive styrofoam coolers at a local supermarket, which in combination with ice bags make an excellent ice chest.

Before embarking on the trip some foods, such as meats or bread, can be frozen and neatly packed in padded envelopes which serve as insulation and maintain the food for many hours. Packing such items as frozen sliced meats, chicken, bread, packets of cheese, etc., need not add much weight to the luggage. The remaining ingredients and utensils for a balanced meal can be purchased at any well-stocked supermarket. These include fruit juice, breakfast cereals, paper plates, plastic bags and cutlery, fresh fruits and vegetables, canned fish, e.g., salmon, kosher-approved sardines and tuna, and milk for those who accept unsupervised milk.

The traveler must bear in mind that not all foods sold in his local supermarket are available throughout the country. In many parts of the country, kosher dairy products – e.g., cottage cheese, sour cream, yogurt, and cheese – are not available. Unlike the East, where plain yogurt is produced solely with cultures, there are areas where it is produced with gelatin, and must be avoided.

Nor should the traveler expect to find such familiar kosher approved items as packaged bread, matzohs, poultry products, gefilte fish, etc., in areas where the Jewish population is minimal.

Certainly a small can of fish with fresh vegetables, juice or milk with a few slices of bread, is adequate nourishment and far better than subsisting on candy bars and soda. While the traveler may have to forgo the pleasures of home-cooked food in favor of meals prepared *a' la motel,* there is certainly no need for hunger or poor diet as long as one is willing to invest a minimum of time and effort. These procedures may seem strange at first, but after mastering them, kosher travelers will find that they can move about anywhere in the United States without concern for food supply, and be satisfied that they have not compromised their religious standards.

When traveling abroad, the ability to maintain the food supply is more difficult than in the United States, and considerable preparation and thoughtful planning are required. Well-stocked supermarkets are not always available. The many basic kosher-approved prepared foods that are readily available in the United States may be non-existent in many foreign countries. Some of these foods bearing the same brand names as popular United States kosher-approved varieties are kosher only in the Unites States, and not kosher-approved when produced elsewhere.

In many foreign countries it is difficult to establish a system of production where the uniformity can be relied upon, and ingredient lists should not be accepted as a guide. All prepared foods may be suspect of adulteration. In most countries the food industry makes little note of the needs of the Jewish community. Many common food items — condiments, fats, oil, margarine, baked goods, etc. — are not available kosher-approved. It is essential that the committed traveler gain first-hand information from the responsible authorities within the local Jewish community as to what foods and food services may be obtained.

Behind the Iron Curtain, kashruth difficulties are even more compounded. When traveling in countries controlled by Communist regimes, one must be very circumspect before accepting the guarantees of government-appointed religious functionaries.

In many countries of the world, government standards for agricultural control are insufficient and ineffectual. Even authorities that permit the consumption of general-production milk in the United States do not maintain this opinion in countries where agricultural and dairy control is weak and poorly regulated. This is especially so in areas where it is common for farmers to milk their mares or camels. (Supervised milk is discussed in the chapter "Dairy.")

Another danger is the tendency to accept the reliability of kashruth hearsay when being told that "they say" that the bread or some other food in a particular place is kosher. This type of information should be regarded as idle rumor unless substantiated by the kashruth guarantee of experts.

Some travelers arrange for kosher airline meals to be shipped with their luggage to their hotels. These arrangements require clearance from the airline for shipment and from the hotel for storage of the meals in the hotel freezer. Such meals are sealed and double wrapped in foil, and may then be warmed in the hotel ovens and delivered by room service with seals intact.

Other travelers simply pack tinned and non-perishable food items with their luggage, and improvise meals in this fashion.

When traveling in Israel, unfortunately, one cannot assume that all foods are acceptable, unless they are authentically kashruth guaranteed. Not only is the ingredient content and source of food a factor, but kashruth scrutiny must be given to all fruits and vegetables which require *hafrashas matanos* (tithing). In addition to the universal kashruth guarantees, the taking of the tithes (*trumos* and *maaseros)* must be attested to as well. It is essential that before embarking on such a trip, one seek out the guidance of expert authorities to learn firsthand how to perform this *mitzvah,* and how to determine the effectiveness of the kashruth guarantees.

Kosher travelers should be aware that, as an added security measure, many hotels, both in the United States and overseas, have installed electronic door locks that are opened with punch cards or plates. These devices may not be used on *Shabbos* or *Yom Tov.* When travelers make arrangements to stay in hotels over these periods, it is necessary to investigate the type of locks used and avoid such hotels.

The Challenge of Business and Social Obligations

A critical test of kashruth conditioning is the ability to remain fully observant when confronted with the challenges of business and social obligations. Unlike the difficulties encountered while traveling where one still remains in full control, the atmosphere of business and social life creates pressure for kashruth compromise. This is especially true where there are either no kosher facilities or where those that are available are inadequate for business needs.

Entertaining clients, or being entertained by them; business meetings, conventions and seminars; and social gatherings of business acquaintances are all part of the American way of doing business. Unless met with discipline and control, these challenges can become the vehicle for kashruth and religious laxity. It is vital for observant Jews to realize the need to maintain an inner self-respect and consistency of religious behavior under all conditions. This wholehearted commitment is the basis for the strength to avoid temptation to compromise at home and in business and social situations. In order to establish honest religious consistency, there is need for serious soul searching when faced with critical circumstances, and a willingness to accept the truth regardless of the difficulty.

Many businessmen are familiar with friends and associates who have set comfortable self-serving guidelines based solely on the imagery of a kashruth mirage. Some of the more common versions of this unfortunate practice permit eating pastry and other foods in non-kosher dairy or vegetarian restaurants and health food establishments. Such spurious claims ignore the fact that unless a facility is kashruth controlled, it must be assumed that many non-kosher food items — including non-kosher fish, cheese, oils, margarines, mixes, condiments, wines and a full variety of non-kosher ingredients — are used. Some such restaurants have been in existence for many years, successfully using non-kosher ingredients to cater to Jewish ethnic tastes and cuisine.

Worse yet is the practice of some of these facilities to make use of their popularity by producing under their names a line of Jewish ethnic-packaged foods with kosher endorsement, leaving the unwitting to assume that the restaurant bearing the same name and serving the same types of food is kosher as well.

Another illusory standard permits eating of selected foods in non-kosher restaurants. For various unfounded reasons this special permissiveness will permit the otherwise observant patron to eat fish, smoked fish, and a variety of vegetable dishes and pastry, without giving thought to the source of supply and the method of preparation. The smoked fish may have been prepared in a non-kosher facility where it was smoked and cured with non-kosher fish. Fish prepared in a non-kosher kitchen must be assumed to be non-kosher, having been prepared with foods and utensils that are non-kosher. Vegetable dishes, too, come in contact with non-kosher knives, boards and other utensils which are not free of the residue of non-kosher foods.

In truth there are few options in a non-kosher facility. Some restaurants will accommodate kosher clientele with either a can of fish or a serving of whole vegetables and fruit; others may offer kosher pre-cooked airline-type dinners.

Truly committed Jews recognize the difficulties they encounter and treasure the rewards of their religious integrity.

Commerce with Forbidden Foods*

The Talmud states that the Torah prohibits not only the consumption of the forbidden species (animal, fowl, fish and insects), but it also prohibits Jews from engaging in commerce and trade with these commodities, even if they are being sold exclusively to non-Jews. Included in the prohibition is the flesh of *treifah* or not-ritually-slaughtered animals of the permitted species. This prohibition is limited

* The laws of this section are discussed in *Yoreh Deah* 117.

to foods which the Torah forbids. However, it is permitted to engage in trade with foods restricted by Talmudic law.

The Talmud further states that trade is forbidden with the livestock of the non-kosher species that are raised primarily for food. Animals whose primary uses are as beasts of burden or pets, e.g., horses, donkeys, dogs, cats, may be bought and sold. Nor is there any restriction on the sale of forbidden foods that came inadvertently into one's possession or became non-kosher, during the process of kosher-slaughtering, or was found to be *treifah* or in a net used to catch fish, where non-kosher species were caught as well. Such meat or fish may be sold provided that it is clearly identified as non-kosher.

The Torah restriction of trade with forbidden foods includes food service, catering, wholesaling, concessions, etc., as well. Consequently, individuals engaged in these occupations must consult with expert authorities for guidance.

T'vilas Kailim (Immersion of Vessels)

The Mitzvah*

Since this volume is intended to serve as an effective introductory guide to kashruth observance and the proper management of the kosher home, it would not be complete without a section on the *mitzvah* of *t'vilas kailim*

* The laws of this section are discussed in *Yoreh Deah* 120.

In this section we have described some of the details for the performance of the *mitzvah* of *t'vilah* based upon the decisions found in the various responsa and the volume *T'vilas Kailim* by Rabbi Zvi Cohen (Bnai Brak, 1974). Since our work is a simple outline, the reader should seek the guidance of competent authorities in order to accurately fulfill the mitzvah.

— the immersion of food utensils in a *mikvah,* or in other waters fit for the *mitzvah* of *t'vilah,* such as a well or the ocean. This *mitzvah* is to be performed upon the transfer of utensils from non-Jewish ownership to Jewish ownership, as described in the Torah: "As far as the gold, silver, copper, iron, tin and lead are concerned, whatever was used over the fire must be brought over fire and purged, and (then) purified with the sprinkling water. However, that which was not used over fire need only be immersed in a *mikvah*" (*Numbers* 31:22,23). However, utensils produced under Jewish ownership and remaining under Jewish ownership until they reach the consumer do not require immersion.

In order to insure that the *mitzvah* is carried out properly, the matter should be reviewed in detail with experienced, competent authorities. When the *mitzvah* is performed, a blessing is recited before the vessel is immersed.

The *mitzvah* of *t'vilas kailim* attests to the sanctity of the Jewish nation. Not only are we to regard our bodies and souls as sacred, but our possessions as well. The utensils with which we prepare our food are, therefore, to be sanctified by immersion in a *mikvah* — a *mitzvah* that is an eternal reminder of the holy purpose of life and of *Am Yisroel.*

The *mitzvah* should be performed before the utensils are put into use. In the case of non-kosher utensils they should first be koshered, and then immersed. Food that was prepared in kosher utensils that were not immersed is nonetheless kosher, and may be eaten.

The *mitzvah* requires that the entire vessel be immersed in the water at one time. Therefore, care must be taken when immersing vessels with narrow openings, that the interior be filled with water either before or during the total immersion. Similarly, the vessel must be thoroughly clean and free from any foreign matter. Product labels, price tags, adhesives, and anything that is not a permanent part of the utensil must be removed before performing the *mitzvah*.

Not all materials are included in the *mitzvah,* since the Torah enumerates only utensils made of metal. Wood, rubber, stone, earthenware, ivory, plastic and other man-made materials do not require *t'vilah.*

(The blessing recited before immersing vessels in the *mikvah* is, "...אֲשֶׁר קִדְּשָׁנוּ בְּמִצְוֹתָיו וְצִוָּנוּ עַל טְבִילַת כֵּלִים." If only one vessel is immersed the word כֵּלִי is used instead of כֵּלִים.)

Utensils Used in Preparing Food

Glassware, Enamel, China

Glassware, although it is also earthenware and not mentioned in the Torah, is an exception, and requires *t'vilah* by Talmudic law, since it is a molten material similar to metal. Pyrex, Duralex and Corelle are glass, and, as such, these utensils require *t'vilah* as well.

The status of enamel is the subject of Rabbinic responsa; most authorities maintain that the *t'vilah* should be performed, but that the blessing is not recited.

Since porcelain/china is an earthenware product and not a molten material, many authorities maintain that *t'vilah* is not necessary, as earthenware is exempted from the mitzvah. Others are of the opinion that since these utensils are glazed, *t'vilah* should be performed without the recitation of the blessing.

Throw-Away Utensils

Many authorities maintain that metal utensils such as aluminum foil trays or pans, which are discarded after use, do not have the significance of household utensils, and *t'vilah* is not required.

Coated Utensils

Many pots and pans are produced with coatings such as Teflon, etc. These too are the subject of discussion and commentary, and have special requirements regarding the *mitzvah* of *t'vilah*, since plastic is a material which does not require *t'vilah*.

Consequently, metal pots and pans that are coated on the inside with Teflon or other types of non-*t'vilah* materials should be immersed and the blessing not recited.

If these pots are coated with non-*t'vilah* materials only on the outside, or if the inside coating is strictly for decorative purposes, then *t'vilah* is required with the blessing.

For non-*t'vilah* materials that are coated with metal, i.e., plastic bowls with metal linings, the procedure is somewhat more complex. When non-*t'vilah* materials are coated on both sides with metal, *t'vilah* with a blessing is required. When metal is on the interior only, or even on both sides but solely for decorative purposes, then *t'vilah* is required and the blessing is recited.

For utensils that are coated with glass both inside and out for non-decorative purposes, *t'vilah* is required without a blessing.

When a non-*t'vilah* material is covered only externally with metal, or metal parts are attached to the outside (handles, etc.), no *t'vilah* is required.

Serving Trays and Warmers

The *mitzvah* of *t'vilah* is limited to glass and metal vessels that come in direct contact with food and are used for preparation, serving and eating. Hot plates and containers that are used to warm covered foods or containers, and thus do not come in direct contact with the food, do not require *t'vilah*. Similarly, candy dishes and serving plates that are used exclusively to serve wrapped foods do not require *t'vilah*. In the case of appliances that are used to prepare food that will require further processing, i.e., meat grinders, dough mixers, etc., there is discussion as to whether they are included in the *mitzvah.* In these instances, the *t'vilah* is performed without the ritual blessing.

Electrical Appliances

Electrical appliances that come in direct contact with the food present a unique problem. Since they are made of metal, they should require *t'vilah*, yet many such appliances may be damaged if they are totally immersed in water. Most authorities maintain that electrical appliances are similar to all other cooking and baking utensils, and *t'vilah* is required. Some are of the opinion that since the electrical unit cannot be operated unless it is plugged into the wall outlet, it loses the status of a vessel; rather it should be considered as part of the building similar to the wall to which it is attached, and *t'vilah* is not necessary.

Often the parts of the electrical appliance that come in contact with the food are detachable, such as the mixing bowls, beaters, kneaders, blender knives, grates, and pans. If so, only the parts that come in contact with the food need be removed and immersed.

Other electrical appliances, e.g., percolators, etc., which require *t'vilah*, and may be damaged by the water if fully immersed, are the subject of responsa. Most authorities maintain that since a utensil which was constructed by a Jew requires no *t'vilah*, it follows that if the utensil was disassembled and then reassembled by a Jewish craftsman, the appliance is considered of Jewish construction, and *t'vilah* is not necessary. However, these authorities point out that simple reassembly requiring no special skills cannot give the utensil the status of having been made by a

Jew, and *t'vilah* is required. Another practical solution is that, when possible, the electrical unit, wires, contact points, etc., that could be damaged by water, be removed before *t'vilah*, and reinserted after the *mitzvah* has been performed.

Temporary Situations

In a situation where *t'vilah* is temporarily impossible, such as on a Sabbath when it is forbidden to perform the *mitzvah,* or where one is traveling in an area where there is no access to a *mikvah,* well or ocean, there is a method by which one may use the utensil without *t'vilah*. The utensil may be given to a non-Jew as a gift, and then borrowed from him. Since it is owned by a non-Jew, the utensil may be used without *t'vilah*. Many authorities point out that this is only a temporary measure, but the permanent use of such a utensil over a long period of time would indicate ownership, and the *t'vilah* should be performed, though the blessing need not be recited.

Some maintain that in case of electrical appliances that cannot be immersed without damage, the appliance may be given to a non-Jew as a gift, then borrowed, and may be used thereafter without *t'vilah*.

Asking Questions

Kashruth observers are aware that even in the presence of a sound Torah background and organized system of religious life, numerous questions arise related to kashruth and Torah practice. In commonplace daily life, errors occur as a result of spills, mix-ups and oversights. People should take the trouble to ask competent authorities regarding these halachic questions. Those who rely on their own often superficial knowledge may be using utensils and eating foods that are forbidden, or — surprisingly — may be throwing away food and utensils that are permitted.

Too often we fall into the habit of consulting with learned experts only in an emergency, at which time it may be impossible to benefit from the full detail of their learned expertise. In order to obtain a fuller and more accurate understanding of religious practice, it is essential that each individual seek out competent authorities for guidance, and discuss these topics with them on a regular basis. This is especially important since constant change often raises new questions in kashruth and other areas of life. By establishing an ongoing relationship with such authorities we create the opportunity of availing ourselves of knowledge that only personal contact imparts, and which enables us to glean expertise that we could not otherwise obtain.

The observant Jew need not be ashamed to ask even seemingly simple questions of such authorities, and we should bear in mind the motto, "The only foolish question is the one that is not asked." Certainly this is a better policy than to rely on the unlearned opinions of friends, neighbors and storekeepers whose information is often based on inaccurate hearsay or self-interest.

The regular contact with learned experts is a key to true Torah observance. It is not only imperative to seek counsel when mistakes are made, but necessary to maintain a direct personal relationship with Torah authorities. It is then that the individual will fully realize that matters relating to the methods of koshering utensils, foods prepared in improper utensils, ingredient contents, the reliability of kashruth guarantees, and many more questions of Torah observance and daily religious life require thorough training, erudite knowledge and experience before a decision can be rendered. Certainly the rewards of knowledge and reassurance to be gained are worth the small investment of time and effort.

Additives

The consumer is often confronted with food product ingredients whose origin and kashruth acceptability are difficult for the average individual to trace. This section on food additives has been prepared to help eliminate this confusion and to provide better understanding. It includes the most common additives used in the United States.

In addition to a brief description of the additive, we have also pointed out the various food products in which it is most often used. A careful study of this section will provide the kashruth observer with the rudiments of a technical kashruth background.

It is our hope that through a better understanding of food components, their function and derivation, the consumer will be able, at a glance, to identify kashruth problems, and make a knowledgeable selection of kosher foods.

ACACIA – see GUM ARABIC

ACEROLA

Acerola is obtained from a cherry-like fruit which grows in the Caribbean area and parts of Florida. It is widely regarded as one of the richest natural sources for vitamin C, and is used as a nutritional supplement.

ACETIC ACID (VINEGAR)

Acetic acid is synthetically produced from petrochemicals, and in its undiluted state is referred to as galacial acetic acid. Acetic acid may be produced naturally by the fermentation of cane sugar, cider, glucose, the different varieties of alcohol (i.e., petroleum, grain, citrus, wine). Natural acetic acid is referred to as vinegar, and identified by its source, i.e., grain vinegar, wine vinegar and so on. When it is added to a food product, however, the source of the vinegar need not be identified on the food label. Chemically produced acetic acid when used in a food product is identified by the term acetic acid, since it is not natural fermented vinegar.

Acetic acid/vinegar is used in foods as an acid flavoring agent, especially in ketchup, mayonnaise, dressings, marinades, and pickles. In addition, acetic acid is an effective anti-microbial preservative, and therefore widely used in the production of processed meats. It is also compounded with other chemicals to produce acetates (e.g., sodium diacetate, calcium diacetate), which are preservatives used to inhibit the growth of mold and bacteria in baked goods and fillings.

Products containing vinegar must be kashruth controlled to guarantee both the origin of the vinegar as neither wine nor wine alcohol, and that the vinegar product was not produced in common with these types of vinegar.
(See also ETHANOL.)

ADIPIC ACID

Adipic acid occurs naturally in beets and is commercially

produced synthetically from petrochemicals.

Adipic acid is used in gel desserts, beverage powders, flavorings, jams and jellies, baking powder and processed dairy products as an acidulant imparting a smooth, tart taste.

AGAR

Agar alginates are produced from algae seaweed that have been dried and processed. Some ingredient lists may refer to it generically as a hydrophilic colloid, or to its original Malayan name, agar-agar.

Since agar is a resilient, clear gelling agent it is used in baked goods, toppings, candies, powdered desserts, meat, fish and dairy products. As with all gums, when used in combination with other gums it may be indicated as vegetable gum.

ALDEHYDES – see FLAVORS

ALGINATES

Alginates are produced from varieties of algae (seaweed) and used as gelling and stabilizing agents in beverages, frozen confections, baked goods, meats, dairy products, dressings, jams, jellies and toppings.
(See also AGAR; KELP; CARRAGEENAN.)

AMBERGRIS – see FLAVORS

ANNATO-BIXIN – see FOOD COLORING

ASCORBIC ACID (VITAMIN C)

Ascorbic acid is commercially derived from dextrose by a fermentation process which converts the dextrose into ascorbic acid (Krebs cycle).

In addition to its value as a nutritional supplement, ascorbic acid is used as an anti-oxidant food preservative in fats, oils, processed meats and fish, dairy products, beverages and baked goods.
(See also DEXTROSE.)

ASCORBYL PALMITATE

Ascorbyl palmitate is produced from ascorbic acid and palmitic acid. Palmitic acid is a fatty acid of either vegetable or animal origin. It is used as a preservative for fats and oils.

Ascorbyl palmitate must be produced under effective kashruth control in order to guarantee the source and process of the palmitic acid.

(See also ASCORBIC ACID; STEARIC ACID.)

ASPARTIC ACID

Aspartic acid is found in animals and plants, and is especially abundant in sugar cane and beet molasses. It is most commonly produced synthetically by the enzymatic microbial process with mineral chemicals.

In addition to pharmaceutical uses, aspartic acid is used in the production of synthetic sweeteners (aspartame).

AZO DYES — see FOOD COLORING

BAKING SODA — see SODIUM BICARBONATE

BETA CAROTENE

Beta carotene is present in many plants and is derived from either carrot or palm oil by extraction, or by microbial processing of corn and soybean oil.

Beta carotene is used as a coloring agent in foods for deep orange/yellow pigment. Beta carotene is most commonly used as a coloring agent for butter, cheese, margarine and shortenings. Since the human body transforms carotene into vitamin A it is also added to many foods as a nutritional supplement. The finished beta carotene product is produced either in the natural oil form or impregnated into gelatin beadlets.

(See also ENCAPSULATION; GELATIN.)

BHA (BUTYLATED HYDROXYANISOLE)

BHA is produced from petrochemical derivatives, and used in fats and oils to prevent rancidity, and as a food preservative in many processed foods.

It is often added to the food-packaging material and acts to preserve the food contained in the packaging thereby extending the shelf life of the product.

BHT (BUTYLATED HYDROXYTOLUENE)

BHT is produced from either petroleum or coal tar derivatives; and is used to prevent rancidity in fats and oils. In chewing-gum base it aids in maintaining the softness and chewability; and is used as a preservative in many foods.

BHT is also added to food-packaging material and acts to preserve the food contained within, thereby extending the shelf life of the product.

BROMATE

Bromates are derived from natural salts that are further processed with other minerals and chemicals to produce either calcium or potassium bromate.

They are most commonly used in flour as a maturing agent (brominated flour) and as a dough conditioner.

BROMELAIN — see ENZYMES

CAFFEINE

Caffeine is the natural extract of coffee, tea or kola nuts, and is used as an additive in beverages.

CALCIUM BROMATE — see BROMATE

CALCIUM CARBONATE

Calcium carbonate is a natural mineral. It is mined and processed by the chemical process of combining calcium chloride and sodium carbonate.

It is added to cereal, flour, bread, baked goods, candies, confections and many other foods. Surface modified calcium carbonates have been developed. These are produced with coatings bonded to the particles of powder, in order to insure the even dispersion of the calcium carbonate. The material used for the bonding is either resin or stearates.

Bonded types of calcium carbonates must be effectively

kashruth controlled to guarantee the source of the coatings. (See also ENCAPSULATION.)

CALCIUM STEARATE / MAGNESIUM STEARATE

Calcium stearate is produced by interacting stearic acid with calcium chloride.

It is used as an anti-caking agent to keep powders free flowing, especially in such products as garlic and onion salt; some specialty powdered sugars; spice blends; powdered coffee creamers; and malted milk powders. It is also used in the production of pharmaceutical tablets and as a lubricant in food production.

In some processes the stearates are interacted with magnesium to produce magnesium stearates, which are also used as lubricants and anti-caking agents.

Since calcium stearates and magnesium stearates are produced with stearic acid of animal or vegetable origin, kashruth can be guaranteed only when manufacture is under full and effective kashruth control.
(See also STEARIC ACID.)

CALCIUM STEAROYL LACTYLATE — see STEAROYL LACTYLATE

CARAMEL — see FOOD COLORING

CARBOXYMETHYCELLULOSE (CELLULOSE GUM)

CMC (Carboxymethycellulose) was originally developed as a substitute for gelatin and is produced from the cellulose of wood pulp or cotton linters that are chemically treated and reacted with sodium hydroxide and chloroacetic acid.

CMC is widely used as a stabilizer in ice cream, frozen confections, fillings, toppings, puddings, and salad dressings. It is used as a bulking agent and moisturizer in baked goods.

CARMINE — see FOOD COLORING

CARRAGEENAN

Carrageenan is a gum derived from several varieties of

algae (seaweed) found in North America, Europe, and North Africa. The gum is extracted from the weeds with hot water, and further purified by drying or alcohol precipitation.

It is used as a gelling agent, stabilizer and thickener in fillings, desserts, frozen confections, salad dressings, soups, syrups, toppings, dessert gels, dairy products, and as a clarifier in beer.

CASEIN

Casein is a combination of several proteins that form the major portion of the protein content of milk. It is produced by treating milk, either by adding acid to skim milk or by adding rennet. The acid-precipitated protein is used primarily for food products. The rennet casein (paracasein) is also used for adhesives, laminates, and other industrial products.

Casein is used as a dairy protein additive in the preparation of imitation dairy products, i.e., coffee whiteners, drinks, powdered beverages, cheese, ice cream, frozen confections, candies, baked goods. Hydrolyzed casein is used as a flavor enhancer in many processed foods. It may also be used to inhibit the formation of crystals in canned albacore tuna.

Kashruth control is necessary to guarantee the method and source materials used in the production of casein.

(See also HYDROLIZED VEGETABLE PROTEINS; RENNIN.)

CASTOREUM — see FLAVORS

CATALASE — see ENZYMES

CELLULOSE GUM — see CARBOXYMETHYCELLULOSE

CITRIC ACID

Citric acid is commercially produced by means of enzymatic conversion of corn flour into syrup, and then further treating the syrup with micro-organisms which convert the corn syrup into citric acid. It is also produced by a similar process from molasses.

Citric acid is a natural preservative and acts as an anti-oxidant, retarding browning and spoilage, and is therefore added to canned fruits, vegetables, juices, fillings, fish products, fats and oils. It is widely used as an acidulant and flavor additive in beverages, fruit preserves, confections, cheese and dairy products, relishes, sauces and wine.
(See also MOLASSES.)

CIVET — see FLAVORS

CMC — see CARBOXYMETHYCELLULOSE

COCHINEAL — see FOOD COLORING

COCOA BUTTER

Cocoa butter is the fat produced from cocoa beans, and is used in the preparation of chocolate confections.

CORN SYRUP

Corn syrup is produced from corn starch by conversion of the starch into corn sugar by either hydrolysis or enzymatic action. When the enzymatic action is continued, the corn syrup can be further processed into dextrose and fructose.

In addition to its sweetening properties, corn syrup inhibits crystallization when used in foods. Corn syrup is used as the syrup for canned fruits, jams, jellies, ice creams, candy, beverages, condiments, baked goods, and many other processed foods.
(See also DEXTROSE; FRUCTOSE.)

CREAM OF TARTAR (TARTARIC ACID)

Cream of tartar is obtained from the stony sediment that is formed in wine barrels. After aging and baking or drying, the sediments are purified by an acid-and-alkali treatment, and ground into fine powder. Another process for producing tartrates is the boiling in water of press cakes left from the production of grape juice. The hot mash is permitted to settle, and the clear liquid is cooled and crystallized.

Cream of tartar is used in baking powder as a leavening

agent and as a source material for tartaric acid, which is used as an enhancer in fruit flavors, preserves, and confections.

When cream of tartar is produced by the aging/baking/drying and acid-and-alkali process, the wine residue is dissipated in the sediment, and the product is kosher. Kashruth guarantees are necessary to confirm the manufacturing procedure.

CYSTEIN

Cystein is produced by hydrolysis from keratin, the protein found in hair and feathers.

Cystein is used to improve the quality of bread dough, speed the baking process, and as a nutritional supplement in vitamin preparations. It now has been found to be useful as a flavor ingredient in processed flavors.

DEXTRIN

Dextrin is produced from food starch, either by heating the starch, treating it with acids, or by chemical conversion.

Dextrin starches are used as coatings in chewing gum and candies; and in the production of fried potatoes, processed meats, snack foods, dried beverages and food-mix formulations.

DEXTROSE, GLUCOSE

Dextrose is a form of glucose, a basic sugar. In the United States, it is most commonly produced from cornstarch by an enzymatic process which converts the starch into corn syrup. Then, by continuous conversions, the syrup is converted to pure dextrose sugar. In other parts of the world, wheat and potato starch are commonly used to produce dextrose.

Dextrose is widely used in many foods — including baked goods, candy confections, beer, infant-food preparations, canned foods, pharmaceuticals — and is the starting material for the manufacture of vitamin C.
(See also CORN SYRUP.)

DISODIUM INOSINATE — see INOSINIC ACID

EDTA (ETHYLENEDIAMINETETRAACETIC ACID)

EDTA is produced from tetrasodium and other chemicals of mineral origin.

EDTA is a chelating agent which traps the trace metals present in foods and beverages and prevents them from discoloring, clouding, or causing rancidity. It is used as a preservative in beverages, dressings, margarine, fruit juices, and processed fruits and vegetables.

ENCAPSULATION

Encapsulation is a process by which the powder particles of an ingredient are coated with a protective layer. This coating aids in the handling and better use of the product. Encapsulated ingredients are able to maintain their stability, and in some instances, encapsulation makes possible the gradual release of an ingredient when it is combined in a mixture.

Some of the coatings used for encapsulation are vegetable fats, sugar, starch, glyceride emulsifier, gelatin, and whey protein.

Among the many products now available in the encapsulated form are calcium carbonate, citric acid, food colors, vitamins, spray-dried flavors, lactic acid, and salt.

In each instance, effective kashruth control is necessary to guarantee the source and process of the encapsulation. (See also HYDROGENATED VEGETABLE SHORTENING; GELATIN; GLYCERIDES; WHEY.)

ENOCIANINA — see FOOD COLORING

ENZYMES

Enzymes are a natural substance produced by living cells, and occur naturally in many foods. Fermented foods, such as wine, beer and bread, are examples of the action of enzymes.

For industrial use, enzymes are added to foods under

controlled conditions to bring about specific reactions. Enzymes are obtained from plants, animal tissue and microbial sources for commercial use.

The most common plant enzymes are malt amylase, papain, ficin, and bromelain. These are derived from barley malt, papaya, figs and pineapple. In addition to these, micro-organisms have been found to produce abundant amounts of enzymes, and these are referred to as microbial enzymes.

Plant and microbial enzymes are used extensively to convert starch into sugar and syrup; added to flour to improve dough quality; in the fermentation of grains, and as meat tenderizers. Invert sugar, corn syrup, dextrose and fructose are all results of enzymatic action.

Pectic enzymes produced from fungi are used extensively in the processing of apple, grape, berry and other fruit juices, concentrates, purees and wine. These enzymes aid and increase the rapid release of the juices from the fruit.

Among the enzymes derived from animal tissue are pepsin, rennet, lipase and catalase.

Rennet plays a major role in the production of cheese and dairy products. When added to milk it forms the curd from which cheese is made, and brings about the reactions which give each type of cheese its unique characteristics. In recent years enzymes produced by microbial means have been introduced for use in the production of cheese and dairy products.

Oral lipases extracted from the glands at the base of the tongue of animals are employed to bring about reactions in butter fat, and create unique flavor sensations. These fats are referred to as having been lipolized. Lipolized cream and butter-fat flavors are used in margarines, butter sauces, vegetable oil, chocolate and caramel confections, processed cheese products, and imitation dairy products, as well as a variety of pharmaceuticals. Microbial enzymes have been developed which duplicate the action of natural lipase. Lipases extracted from the pancreas are used as digestive aids and added to commercial egg whites to aid in removal of yolk particles, to enhance the whipping qualities.

Products produced with enzymes must be effectively kashruth controlled in order to guarantee the source and process of the enzymatic material.

ESTER GUM — see GLYCERYL ABIETATE

ESTERS — see FLAVORS; SORBITAN

ETHANOL (ETHYL ALCOHOL)

Ethanol or ethyl alcohol is most often produced either by natural fermentation and distillation of grains, or synthetically from petrochemicals. Ethanol is also produced by the fermentation of molasses or citrus fruits.

In wine-producing countries, ethyl alcohol is produced by distilling wine and retrieving the alcohol. This alcohol is used in the production of brandy and cognac, as the alcohol base in flavored liqueurs, and to fortify the alcoholic content of other wines. These alcohols are exported for use in industrial and food production. Some dairy-producing areas have developed facilities for the production of alcohol from milk by-products.

In addition to alcoholic beverages, ethyl alcohol has many uses as a food ingredient, and as a solvent in the preparation of food ingredients, flavorings, detergents, pharmaceuticalsand vinegar.

Products produced with alcohol require effective guarantees to establish the origin of the alcohol used.

FERROUS GLUCONATE — see FOOD COLORING

FIBRIN — see PHENYLALANINE

FICIN — see ENZYMES

FLAVORS — ARTIFICIAL AND NATURAL

A flavor formulation may consist of many substances, some natural and others synthetic. These flavor chemicals are unique in that they impart flavor characteristics similar to those of the natural food product, and can be blended with other natural or synthetic materials to create either flavors similar to those found in nature or new flavor sensations.

Under the law, when flavor ingredients are added to a food product, the declaration on the label must indicate that flavor has been added, since the flavor of the food is not entirely its own, but has been enhanced.

There are more then fifteen hundred flavor ingredients – both of natural extract and synthetic chemicals – that may be used in the preparation of a formula. The chemicals are referred to as acids, alcohols, aldehydes, esters, ketones, or thiols. They are produced by a synthetic chemical process, either from fats and oils of animal or vegetable origin, or from petrochemicals. In addition there are various enzymes and extracts from animal glands and organs that are used as ingredients in flavor formulations.

Some examples are: (a) ambergris – an extract of a growth from sperm whale intestines which has been found to possess blending qualities; (b) castoreum – an extract of beaver glands used to enhance berry-type flavors; (c) civet – produced from the secretion of the civet cat, and used to blend flavor ingredients, or for its effect on cheese and alcoholic flavors; (d) lipase – an enzyme derived from calf glands used in dairy products, as well as butter- and cheese-flavored foods.

When these are produced synthetically there must be effective kashruth control to insure the source and procedure.

Flavor formulations may also contain a variety of fruit extracts and concentrates including grape, wine and cognac to enhance fruit-type flavors.

In addition to the flavor ingredients, solvents must be added to the formula in order for the product to properly dilute and uniformly maintain its qualities in the food or beverage to which it is added. Most commonly used for this purpose are propylene glycol (a petrochemical derivative), glycerin (either animal or synthetic), ethyl alcohol (ethanol) and water. In some formulae, polysorbates (of either animal or vegetable origin) are added to increase the water solubility of the flavor.

The kosher status of a flavor formulation, either natural or artificial, can be determined only after review of all flavor ingredients, solvents, vehicles; and effective kashruth control of the flavor preparation.

(See also ETHANOL; GLYCERIN; POLYSORBATES.)

FOOD COLORING

Food colorings listed as FD&C (an abbreviation of Food, Drug and Cosmetics) certified color are added to foods by approval granted by the Food and Drug Administration under the Federal Food, Drug, and Cosmetic Act first enacted in 1938. Under the Act, standards are set for the certification of each dye or pigment; a specific number is assigned for each color; and the limits of its use as a food and coating color are established. FD&C colors are either coal tar or other chemical/mineral derivatives.

These materials are under constant review by the government, and at the present time nine coloring substances are certified: Yellow 5, Yellow 6, Red 40, Citrus Red 2 and Orange B (all azo dyes); Blue 1 and Green 3 (triphenylmethane dyes); Red 3 (xanthine); and Blue 2 (sulfonated indigo).

Present government regulations permit coloring substances of natural and/or synthetic origin which do not require certification, and therefore, when added to the product, do not indicate "FD&C." Such colorings include:

(a) Annato-bixin — derived from the seeds of the Bixa tree and used to give a yellow, peach or orange color to margarine, butter products, baked goods and beverages.

(b) Caramel — produced by heating sugar to obtain a dark brown color, and most commonly made from liquid corn syrup. Caramel is a widely used food coloring in foods and beverages.

(c) Carmine (carminic acid, cochineal) – coloring that is extracted from the dried bodies of the female insect coccus cacti found in South America and the Canary Islands. Though more expensive then FD&C colors, it is used as a pink and red dye in foods and coatings where the coal tar synthetic dyes are unstable and fade, or by companies which wish to eliminate coal tar dyes from their products.

(d) Carotene – an orange/yellow food coloring, occurring naturally in many vegetables and fruits, is produced commercially by a synthetic process from petrochemicals. It is used to color a variety of foods including margarine, oils, and dairy products. In addition to the liquid form it is also marketed in the form of tiny beads made from gelatin that has been impregnated with carotene. Carotene beadlets are highly soluble and are used in ice cream, puddings, orange flavored beverages and cheeses. (See also ENCAPSULATION.)

(e) Enocianina (grape skin extract) – produced from the skins and pulp residue of grapes (pomace) after the juice has been pressed from them. It is used to give a deep wine-red color to foods, fruit beverages and liqueurs.

(f) Ferrous gluconate – produced from gluconic acid, a dextrose derivative, and used in the production of black olives.

(g) Natural xanthophyll – lutein dipalmitate (lutexan) – a yellowish color extracted from the pigments naturally found in marigolds, grasses, alfalfa and egg yolks.

(h) Spice oils and extracts – extracts of such spices as paprika and turmeric are often used to add color to dressings, pickles, fish and meat products. Glycerides and polysorbates are added to these spice extracts to increase their solubility, and when used in foods the additives need not be listed as ingredients.

Kashruth control is necessary to guarantee both the source of the colorings and its additives.

FRUCTOSE

Fructose occurs naturally in honey and fruits, and is commercially produced by the enzymatic action of dextrose.

The sweetest of the common sugars, fructose is one and a half times as sweet as common table sugar. High fructose syrups are used in soft drinks, canned fruits, frozen desserts, and many other naturally sweetened processed foods.

(See also CORN SYRUP; DEXTROSE.)

FUMARIC ACID

Fumaric acid occurs in many plants, and is prepared commercially from glucose by microbial fermentation and from petrochemicals.

It is used to acidify beverages, baking powders and powdered desserts, and acts as a flavoring agent, and as an anti-oxidant preservative. Because of these qualities fumaric acid is used in pie fillings and gels, sausage, and many other prepared foods.

FURCELLARAN (DANISH AGAR)

Furcellaran is an extract of seaweed found in Scandinavian waters. It is used as a gelling agent in milk, puddings, jams, jellies, bakery fillings and dietetic products.

GELATIN

Gelatin is produced by extracting collagen, a fibrous animal protein, from beef, calf and pork. After soaking and cooking, collagen is filtered, refined and evaporated to obtain the gelatin. Many years ago in the United States, kosher gelatin was produced from kosher-slaughtered and processed calf skins. The supply of this kosher gelatin has long since been exhausted, and the product is no longer produced.

Since gelatin is highly hydrophilic (able to absorb as much as ten times its weight of water) and forms strong viscous gels, it has many uses in foods and pharmaceuticals.

In addition to flavored gelatin desserts, gelatin is used in marshmallows, bakery fillings and chiffons, frozen desserts, ice creams, soft cheese and cheese spreads, yogurt, sherberts and water ices, candy gels, and coatings for tablets and capsules. Gelatin beads are also used to encapsulate flavors, colors, and vitamins for use in food products.

GLUCONA DELTA LACTONE

Glucona delta lactone is a dextrose derivative produced from gluconic acid.

It is used as a food acid and leavening agent in gel and drink powders, as a preservative in processed meats, and in powdered artificial sweeteners.

GLUCOSE — see DEXTROSE

GLUTAMIC ACID — see MSG

GLYCERIDES (MONO- and DI-)

Since glycerides are among the most widely used additives by food processors, it is only by understanding the nature of the product and the full range of its use that the knowledgeable kosher consumer will be able to identify kashruth problems and properly select food items.

Glycerides are produced by "reacting" fats (either animal or vegetable) with glycerin. Glycerin too is a product of either animal or vegetable fats, or is synthetically produced from petroleum derivatives.

Depending upon modifications of the process, the end product is referred to as a mono- or di-glyceride, each of which is defined by the structure of its molecules.

The effects of this additive and the reasons it has become such an important additive in the food industry are as follows:

(a) One of the elementary laws of nature is that oil will not blend with water, and when added to water will rise to the top.

(b) When the mixture is shaken the oil separates into small globules, disperses, and appears to mix with the water. After a short time the oil will rise again to the top just as before, because oil is lighter than water. Moreover, the larger the globule the faster the rate of rise.

(c) By nature each globule of oil is attracted to the next globule and attaches itself to it.

(d) When a glyceride is added to this mixture a barrier is created which prevents the oil globules from attaching themselves to each other. They remain separate and small. The oil, therefore, does not rise to the top. It appears as if the oil and water are mixed. It is, therefore, easy to understand why this product is a basic food additive added to hundreds of foods. One common example of this is coffee whitener which is composed of fats, oil and water. Without the glycerides the fats and oils would rise to the top, and the product would not resemble its dairy cream counterpart. The addition of mono- and di-glycerides makes the mixture stable, and when added to coffee or other liquids the product blends smoothly. The same is true of many other products that require a smooth, moist, creamy texture and complete blending of all ingredients.

Icings, cakes, doughnuts, cake mixes, breads, bread mixes, sour dressings, salad dressings, chocolate, chocolate drinks, candy, chewing gum, ice creams, frozen desserts, coffee creams, baby formulas, margarine, shortenings, oils, flavoring, salt, spices (liquid and dry), pickled products, drink mixes, alcoholic beverages, and vitamin preparations are but a few of the products in which mono- and di-glycerides are a most essential ingredient.

Since glycerides are produced from fats and glycerin of

both animal and vegetable origin, kashruth is guaranteed only when the entire production process, as well as the sources of all raw materials, are under full and effective kashruth control.
(See also GLYCERIN.)

GLYCERIN (GLYCEROL)

Glycerin is produced as a by-product in the refining process of fats and oils, both animal and vegetable, and is synthetically derived from petrochemicals.

Due to its unusual chemical and physical properties as a humectant (i.e., a substance that promotes the retention of moisture), solvent and plasticizer, glycerin is used in hundreds of products and food production processes. Glycerin is a common ingredient in flavor formulations and extracts. Since it adds a smooth quality to the finished product it is commonly used in liqueurs, syrups, and as a base for cough medicines.

Glycerin is a basic ingredient in the production of glycerides, polysorbate emulsifiers and shortenings. It is used to maintain moisture in dried fruits and peels, shredded coconut; as a softener in chewing gum; and in the base of toothpastes and jelly candies. In the production of cellophane and plastic food-wraps and casings, glycerin aids in preventing shrinkage and enhancing the flexibility of the product.

Since glycerin and products containing glycerin are used in many foods and beverages the availability of glycerin from kosher sources is essential to kosher food production. Only when the origin of the glycerin is kashruth guaranteed may the glycerin and products containing glycerin be accepted as kosher.

GLYCERYL ABIETATE / ESTER GUM

Glyceryl abietate may be produced from processed wood resin that has been purified and then reacted with glycerol. Since glycerol is used in the process, only ester gum / glyceryl abietate produced with glycerin of non-animal origin may be accepted as kosher.

Ester gum is most commonly used in orange and other citrus-oil based flavors that are to be used in carbonated and other beverages. The ester gum is a vital ingredient in the production of these flavor emulsions (concentrates). When the ester gum is added to the emulsion it stabilizes and disperses the essential oils, preventing them from rising to the top of the beverage.

[When glyceryl abietate is added to a typical fruit-flavor emulsion, the emulsion will contain approximately three and a half to four parts per hundreds of the ester gum before dilution. This insures that when the emulsion is blended with syrup, then added to the beverage, the total volume of glyceryl abietate in the finished product does not exceed the FDA limit of one hundred parts per million. These figures are based upon the standard of the carbonated beverage industry, wherein five parts of carbonated water are prepared to one part syrup in bottling. These figures may vary, of course, depending upon the nature of the beverage, and the strength of the concentrate.]
(See also GLYCERIN.)

GLYCINE

Glycine is found naturally in gelatin. It is produced commercially by a synthetic chemical process of mineral origin.

Glycine is used in foods as a taste modifier and as a preservative in fats.

GLYCYRRHIZIN

Glycyrrhizin is an extract of the licorice root.

It is intensely sweet and used as a flavoring and foaming agent in beverages such as root beer, in mouth washes, licorice candies, baked goods and confections.

GUANYLIC ACID — see SODIUM GUANYLATE

GUAR GUM

Guar gum is produced from the seed of a bean plant found in India, and now grown in the United States.

Guar gum is used to strengthen the dough of baked goods, to improve the texture of soft cheese, and as a thickening agent in beverages and dressings.

GUM ARABIC

Gum arabic (also called acacia or gum acacia) is derived from the sap of the acacia tree found in Africa. Since gum arabic is one of the most water-soluble gums it is widely used in many foods and beverages as a thickener and stabilizer.

Among them are: candies, jellies, glazes, chewing gum, beer, icings, flavor emulsions, spice blends, wine and baked goods.

GUM GHATTI

Gum ghatti is processed from the sap of a tree found in India.

It is used in beverages and foods as an emulsifier and thickener.

HYDROGENATED VEGETABLE SHORTENING and VEGETABLE OIL

Hydrogenated vegetable shortening is produced from liquid oils that are converted to solid fat by introducing hydrogen under pressure into the oils. In some processes the oil is only partially hydrogenated to retard rancidity and thicken the oil, which remains in its liquid form. This type of product is sold as "vegetable oil," and lists the hydrogenating process as part of the ingredients.

In addition to the hydrogen, glycerides are added to the shortening and oil to enhance their frying and baking qualities. Although glycerides are produced with glycerin and other fatty acids of animal or vegetable origin, they may nevertheless be used even in a "vegetable" oil or shortening product. Similarly, vegetable oil and shortening are often produced at facilities where shortening and oil of animal origin are interchangeably processed.

Vegetable oil and shortening are sold as retail and commercial products, and are used in hundreds of prepared food items, including baked goods, confections, dressings, mayonnaise, margarine and coatings.

Since vegetable oil and shortening may contain non-kosher ingredients or may have been produced in a non-kosher facility, they may be accepted as kosher only when the entire production process and sources of raw materials are under full and effective kashruth control. (See also GLYCERIDES; GLYCERIN.)

HYDROLIZED VEGETABLE PROTEIN (HVP)

Hydrolized vegetable protein is produced by hydrolysis, whereby the proteins of the vegetable flours are isolated. Soy, wheat and other plant flours are commonly used for this purpose. These proteins are then modified to impart meat, fish and poultry-like flavors, or to be used as a flavor enhancer in foods.

HVP is used in processed-meat products, vegetarian-meat flavors, imitation meats, gravy sauces, soup mixes, canned fish, spice blends, soy sauce, oriental foods and flavorings.

In some formulations, fish, meat or casein may be used to produce the hydrolized protein. Such products are referred to as hydrolized proteins, and should not be confused with hydrolized vegetable proteins.

Kashruth guarantees are necessary to insure the sources and production methods of HVP.

HYDROPHILIC COLLOID — see AGAR

INOSINIC ACID (INOSINATE; DISODIUM INOSINATE)

Inosinic acid may be derived from yeast extract, fish and meat, or synthetically from enzymes and microorganisms.

Inosinic acid is a flavor potentiator. It contributes no flavor of its own, but enhances the flavor sensation of the food to which it is added, and has more than ten times the flavor-enhancing ability of MSG.

In addition to enhancing flavor of foods, it increases the "mouthfeel" or body of the product, and is used in spice preparations, soup mixes, processed meats, and in imitation meat and dairy products.

In order to guarantee kashruth, the source materials and production of inosinic acid must be under effective kashruth control.

INVERT SUGAR

Invert sugar is produced from sucrose by enzymatic action or hydrolysis with acids, which splits the sucrose into fifty-percent glucose and fifty-percent fructose, and is sweeter than the cane sugar from which it is derived.

Invert sugar is also a humectant, absorbing and maintaining moisture, and therefore is widely used in candy confections and baked goods.

ISOPROPYL CITRATE

Isopropyl citrate is produced from citric acid reacted with isopropyl alcohol (a petrochemical derivative).

Isopropyl citrate is used as an anti-oxidant in shortening, margarine and oils.
(See also CITRIC ACID.)

KELP

Kelp is produced from algae (seaweed), and is used as a carrier for spices and seasonings in some chewing gum bases, and in the production of alginic acid.

KERATIN — see CYSTEIN

KETONES — see FLAVORS

LACTIC ACID

Lactic acid occurs naturally in many foods and can be produced from corn, soy, cane and beet sugars, whey, or by synthetic process from petrochemical derivatives. In commercial use, the predominant means of lactic acid production is either the fermentation process of sugar or corn starch. It is also produced synthetically from petrochemicals.

Because lactic acid adds a mild flavor and inhibits fermentation, it is used in Spanish-type olives, dried egg powders, vinegar relishes, pickles, fruit juice, some wines, jams, jellies, beer, processed meats and food emulsifiers. It is also added to dry milk powders, baked goods, prepared mixes, fruit pectins, canned fruits, butter and cheese.

LACTOSE (MILK SUGAR)

Lactose is produced from whey, a by-product of cheese.

In addition to many pharmaceutical uses, lactose is added to drink mixes, margarines, infant formulas, dairy products, baked goods and confections. Recently facilities have been developed to produce alcohol from this dairy by-product.

LANOLIN

Lanolin is a waxy substance found in the wool of sheep, and is commonly referred to as wool grease. It is the excretion of the skin glands of the sheep that has been deposited on the wool hairs and is extracted with solvent and processed for use.

Lanolin is used primarily in cosmetics and skin ointments, as well as for edible purposes in chewing gum base, and as the starting material to synthesize 7-dehydrocholesterol from which vitamin D^3 is produced.

Some authorities maintain that since lanolin is exuded from the skin it may be considered identical to body sweat and is permissible.

LARD

Lard is a term used to describe purified hog fat.

Lard is used as a cooking fat and shortening in baked and fried foods. It is either listed as lard or shortening on an ingredient label.

L-CYSTEIN — see CYSTEIN

LECITHIN

Lecithin is a natural emulsifier present in all forms of plant and animal life. For commercial use the predominant source of lecithin is soybean oil. The lecithin is removed during the refining process of the crude oil. Lecithin may also be produced from egg yolks.

Lecithin is added to many oil and food products as an emulsifier, lubricating and anti-splattering agent, anti-oxidant, and stabilizer. It is used in chocolate and chocolate coatings, cream emulsions, cooking sprays, pan coatings, margarine, and many instant food preparations.

Some food processors produce specialty lecithins compounded with other emulsifiers (mono- and di-glycerides) to enhance the properties of the product. Consequently, lecithin products must be kashruth guaranteed to insure the kosher source of the emulsifiers added.

LIPASE — see ENZYMES; FLAVORS

LIPOLIZED FATS — see ENZYMES

LUTEIN DIPALMITATE (LUTEXAN) — see FOOD COLORING

MAGNESIUM STEARATE — see CALCIUM STEARATE

MALIC ACID

Malic acid is found in apples and other fruits, and is produced synthetically for commercial use from petrochemicals.

Malic acid is added to foods as a flavoring agent, preservative and color stabilizer. Among the products to which malic acid is added are fruit-flavored foods, drinks, syrups, fillings, canned tomatoes, jellies, meringues, and candy confections.

MALT

Malt is germinated barley grains. Malt is most commonly produced from barley that has been processed by being steeped in water and partially germinated, then dried.

When a darker color is desired the barley is also scorched.

Malt is used in the brewing of beer, ale, and whiskey, and for the production of malt extract. Malt is rich in carbohydrates, proteins, and enzymes, and is used as a nutritional supplement.

MALT AMYLASE – see ENZYMES

MALT EXTRACT

Malt extract is the concentrate extracted from malt and often combined with glycerol. Malt extract is rich in the enzyme diastase and is used to convert starches into malt sugar; in the brewing process of beer; and as a nutritional supplement in foods.

Malt extract processed with glycerin must be effectively kashruth controlled to guarantee that the source of the glycerin is of kosher mineral or vegetable origin.
(See also GLYCEROL; MALTOSE.)

MALTOL

Maltol occurs naturally in many foods: chicory, treebark, cocoa, coffee, cereals, bread and milk. For commercial use maltol is produced synthetically by the fermentation of vegetable or mineral materials. It is sometimes referred to by the registered mark of a private company as VELTOL.

Though maltol does not contribute any flavor of its own it is used to enhance the flavor of candy, ice cream, desserts, extracts, juices, beverages, puddings, and baked goods.

MALTOSE

Maltose is the sugar produced by the action of the malt enzyme diastase on starch. The enzyme converts the starch into sugar.

Maltose is used as a nutritive sweetener and flavor enhancer in foods and beverages.

MANNITOL (MANNA SUGAR)

Mannitol is common to many plants and readily obtained from seaweed. Since it is abundant in nature and sweet in taste it is sometimes referred to as manna sugar. It is commercially produced by chemical process from corn sugar, glucose or invert sugar.

Because of its ability to absorb and retain moisture, mannitol is used as a humectant (i.e., promoter of moisture absorption and retention), lubricant, and release agent in many foods. It is also used as a flavor carrier and enhancer.

One of the popular uses for mannitol is in sugar-free confections. Since mannitol is not only sweet, but adds bulk to sugar-free products, it is used especially in ice cream, cakes, cookies, and confections. However, mannitol has approximately the same caloric value as sugar.

METHYLPARABEN (PARABENS)

Methylparaben is produced from parahydroxybenzoate, a petrochemical derivative, and is also referred to by the trade name, Parabens.

Methylparaben is used in many food preparations as a preservative to inhibit the growth of mold and bacteria in such foods as cheese, baked goods, soft drinks, beer, syrups, extracts, fruit salads, juices and preserves.

MICROBIAL ENZYMES — see ENZYMES

MODIFIED FOOD STARCH

Modified food starch is derived from chemically treated corn, wheat, potato, rice, tapioca or sago. The processing of modified food starch enables it to be free flowing, preventing cleansing and shearing (the natural breaking down of the starch granules). Thus the starch will maintain its qualities when heated or whipped.

Modified starch is used as an opacifier in beverages, as well as a thickening and emulsifying agent in baked goods, soups, dressings, processed foods and prepared mixes.

In the case of modified starch that is processed by spray drying, kashruth control is necessary since these spray driers may have also been used for other foods.

MOLASSES

Molasses is the syrupy residue produced during the refining process of sugar, and is used as a food flavoring and additive in candy, baked goods, confections, and many processed foods.

Molasses is also used as a nutrient for yeast growth and for starting material in many chemical processes such as the production of citric acid and MSG.

MSG (MONOSODIUM GLUTAMATE; GLUTAMIC ACID)

Monosodium glutamate is produced from vegetable protein of wheat, soy, beet sugar molasses or tapioca; and by synthetic process from petrochemicals.

MSG is a flavor enhancer that intensifies the flavor of the food to which it is added without adding any new flavor of its own. It is widely used in many food preparations and seasoning products, such as soy and other specialty sauces; prepared soup mixes and spice blends; canned, frozen and processed meats, fish and poultry. MSG is sold under various brand names as a retail food flavor additive.

NATURAL FLAVOR – see FLAVORS; OLEORESINS

NIACIN (NICOTINIC ACID)

Niacin is an essential nutrient found in liver, meats, whole grains, fish and yeast. Commercially it is produced synthetically from petrochemical or other mineral sources.

Niacin is used as a nutritional supplement in processed grain products: flour, cereals, noodles, etc., and in vitamin supplements.

(See also VITAMINS.)

OLEORESINS

Oleoresins are the extracts of natural herb and spices. The resin and the essential oil of a spice can be extracted either by solvents, or by a combination of solvent and steam distillation. The approved solvents are hexane, ethylene dichloride, methylene chloride, isopropyl, acetone and ethyl alcohol. After processing, the solvent material is removed from the extract, leaving only a minute acceptable residue.

In addition, certain extract oleoresins must be diluted with vegetable oil and glycerides, which make them soluble when used as a food additive. When oleoresins are used in a food product the ingredient is referred to as either spice oleoresin or extract or natural flavor. The ingredient used for solubility need not be listed.

Oleoresins are highly concentrated and able to be standardized. Food processors often find them more practical in the processing of food products than ground or whole spices.

Since oleoresins are prepared with glycerides and vegetable oils, kashruth is guaranteed only when processed under effective kashruth control.

(See also GLYCERIDES; HYDROGENATED VEGETABLE SHORTENING AND VEGETABLE OIL.)

OXYSTEARIN

Oxystearin is produced from glycerides and stearic acid.

Oxystearin is used as a coating for tablets, and as an anti-crystallization agent in vegetable oils.

Since the components of oxystearin, glycerides and stearic acid are produced from both animal and vegetable sources, the entire production process and sources of the raw materials must be under full and effective kashruth control.

PALMITIC ACID — see ASCORBYL PALMITATE

PAPAIN

Papain is produced from the liquid sap of the papaya fruit.

Papain is a natural protein digestive agent, and is used as a meat tenderizer, and sometimes prescribed as a digestive aid. Papain is also added to beer and other beverages to aid in maintaining their clarity.

PARABENS — see METHYLPARABEN

PARACASEIN — see CASEIN

PECTIC ENZYMES — see ENZYMES

PECTIN

Pectin occurs naturally in many fruits and plants and is derived from the crushed pulp by a heating process or by processing citrus rinds in acid.

Pectin is used as an aid to gel formation in the production of jams, jellies, dessert gels, fruit toppings, and as a thickener in cranberry sauce, dressings, syrups, and beverages. Pectin is often combined with other absorbent substances for use in anti-diarrhea medicines.

PEPSIN

Pepsin is derived from the gastric juices of swine and beef, and is a digestive enzyme.

It is used as an active ingredient in antacid and digestive aid medicines; as a coagulant in the processing of cheese; and as a flavor in some chewing gums.

(See also ENZYMES.)

PHENYLALANINE

Phenylalanine is produced from proteins derived from either egg, fibrin (a blood derivative), grains (zein), milk, or synthetically from silk derivatives.

In addition to pharmaceutical uses, phenylalanine is used in the production of synthetic sweeteners (aspartame).

Kashruth control is necessary to guarantee the source of the phenylalanine.

(See also ZEIN.)

POLYSORBATES

Polysorbates are produced from fatty acids (stearic, oleic, palmitic or lauric). These fatty acids are derived from animal and/or vegetable sources, and processed with sorbitan, a sorbitol derivative. These are then processed with the petrochemical, ethylene oxide, which enables the fatty acid-sorbitan combination to be hydrophilic (blend with water).

Polysorbates are identified universally by a suffix number: 20, 60, 65, 80 and 85. These numerical designations indicate the type of fatty acid (stearic, etc.) used in the manufacturing process. Often polysorbates are referred to by a trade name, TWEEN, which is the registered name of a manufacturer's brand of polysorbates.

Because of the unique qualities of polysorbates, they have many uses in the preparation of foods and food additives, and are often used either by themselves or with other emulsifiers. Among the applications are spice oils, oleoresins, dressings, beverage mixers, non-dairy creamers, coatings, flavorings, powdered and frozen desserts, ice cream and custards, cake mixes, toppings, donut preparations, pickles, relishes and many other foods.

Since polysorbates, like all fatty-acid products, are produced from both animal and vegetable sources, kashruth may be guaranteed only when manufacture is under full and effective kashruth control of all raw materials and the entire production process.

(See also GLYCERIDES; OLEORESINS; SORBITAN FATTY-ACID ESTERS; SORBITOL; STEARIC ACID.)

POTASSIUM BISULFITE — see SULFUR DIOXIDE

POTASSIUM BROMATE — see BROMATE

POTASSIUM META BISULFITE — see SULFUR DIOXIDE

POTASSIUM SORBATE

Potassium sorbate is potassium combined with sorbic acid, a petrochemical derivative.

Because potassium sorbate inhibits both the growth of bacteria and fungi (mold), it is used as a preservative to retard spoilage and rancidity in butter, margarine, mayonnaise, dressings, processed cheese and dairy products, baked goods, pickles, and many other foods and beverages.

POTASSIUM SULFITE — see SULFUR DIOXIDE

PROPIONIC ACID

Although propionic acid occurs naturally in some dairy foods, it is produced commercially from petrochemicals, ethyl alcohol or wood pulp.

Propionic acid is combined with sodium or calcium and is used as a mold inhibitor and preservative in baked goods, and as a chemical flavor additive in the preparation of artificial flavors.

PROPYL GALLATE

Propyl gallate is produced from gallic acid extracted from the tannins of nutgalls of the oak, willow and other trees. The extract is processed with propyl alcohol, a derivative of either grain by-products (fusel oil), other carbohydrate fermentation, or by chemical process from natural gas.

Propyl gallate is used as an anti-oxidant to inhibit the rancidity of fats, oils and foods.

[Note: Propyl alcohol should not be confused with isopropyl alcohol (rubbing alcohol), which is a petrochemical product produced from propylene.]

PROPYLENE GLYCOL

Propylene glycol is derived from petrochemicals.

It is widely used in foods as an emulsifier and solvent in the preparations of flavorings, extracts, liquid spice blends, dressings, fruit syrups; as a mold inhibitor in processed foods and baked goods; and as a humectant (i.e., moisture retainer) to maintain the freshness of dried coconut and other foods.

RENNIN (RENNET)

Rennin is an enzyme produced from the stomach lining of young calves. Rennet is the extract containing the rennin, prepared for commercial use.

Rennet is used to curdle milk in the production of cheese and in some soured dairy products, specialty puddings and yogurts. The rennin derived from the stomach of calves contains the stomach secretions (mucosa) which are natural milk-curdling agents.

Since rennin is a natural enzyme, it is unique in that after clotting the milk, it ceases to act on the curd, and the cheese product produced does not tend to develop a bitter taste.

Rennet substitutes have been developed by microbial means, and milk-clotting enzymes for cheese making are produced from fungi. These microbial enzymes are sometimes referred to as "microbial rennet," though rennet is a term solely for the enzyme derived from the stomach linings of calves.

When rennet is produced from properly kosher-slaughtered, prepared and dried calf stomachs, the rennet extract is permissible for use as a coagulant for kosher cheese products.

(See also CASEIN; ENZYMES.)

RESINOUS GLAZE (SHELLAC)

Shellac is produced from the excretions of the lac insect, which are deposited on various trees in India and South Asia by the lac. The resinous incrustations are scraped from the trees, purified, and blended with alcohol.

Resinous glaze or shellac is a commonly used coating for candies and tablets, which prevents the product from sticking or melting in the hands. Rather than indicating shellac on the ingredient listing, it is referred to as resinous glaze.

Many authorities permit the use of resinous glaze, one of the reasons stated is that shellac is impervious to the acids in the human digestive system, and is not absorbed by the body; thus the eating of resinous glaze may be regarded as similar to eating such undigestible items as wood and stone.

RIBOFLAVIN (VITAMIN B^2)

Riboflavin is found in many foods, i.e., egg yolk, liver, milk, leafy vegetables, yeast. Commercial riboflavin is synthetically produced from a combination of chemical processes involving mineral chemicals or the fermentation of plant or lactose carbohydrates.

Riboflavin is used as a nutritional supplement, and to enrich flour, cereals, and processed food.

SACCHARIN

Saccharin is produced by chemical process from chemicals of mineral origin (ortho-toluenesulfamide).

Saccharin is five hundred times as sweet as sugar and is used as a non-nutritive sweetener and sugar substitute.

SODIUM BICARBONATE (BAKING SODA)

Sodium bicarbonate is a mineral product produced from soda ash.

It is used in baking powder, antacids and other pharmaceuticals.

SODIUM BISULFITE — see SULFUR DIOXIDE

SODIUM CASEINATE — see CASEIN

SODIUM DIACETATE — see ACETIC ACID

SODIUM GUANYLATE (GUANYLIC ACID)

Sodium guanylate or guanylic acid may be derived from yeast extract, fish or meat; or synthetically from enzymes and microorganisms.

Sodium guanylate is a flavor potentiator contributing no flavor of its own, but enhancing the flavor sensation of the food consumed, and has more than ten times the flavor-enhancing ability of MSG.

In addition to enhancing flavor it increases the "mouth-feel" or body of the product, and is therefore used in spice preparations, soup mixes, processed meats, and in imitation meat and dairy products.

In order to guarantee kashruth, the source material and production of guanylic acid must be under effective kashruth control.

SODIUM META BISULFITE — see SULFUR DIOXIDE

SODIUM PYROPHOSPHATE

Sodium pyrophosphate is produced from minerals. It is used in the preparation of baking powders, prepared mixes, and as a preservative for canned and frozen fish.

SODIUM STEAROYL LACTYLATE — see STEAROYL LACTYLATE

SODIUM SULFITE — see SULFUR DIOXIDE

SORBIC ACID

Sorbic acid is derived from petrochemicals. It is used as a food preservative to inhibit mold and bacteria.
(See also POTASSIUM SORBATE.)

SORBITAN FATTY-ACID ESTERS

Sorbitan fatty-acid esters are produced by adding the fatty acids — either stearic, oleic, palmitic or laurel — of both animal and vegetable origin to sorbitan, a sorbitol derivative.

The finished product is often identified to indicate the type of fatty acid used (i.e., sorbitan mono-stearate, sorbitan mono or di-oleate, etc.). The manufacturing process of sorbitan fatty-acid esters does not include the use of ethylene oxide, and therefore the finished product is fat adhering. Often sorbitan fatty-acid esters are referred to by the trademark name SPAN, which is the registered name of a manufacturer's brand of sorbitan fatty-acid esters.

Because of its unique qualities, sorbitan fatty-acids esters are used in many foods and food additives, and in combination with other emulsifiers. Among them are spice oils, oleoresins, bread, cake, and dough mixes, dressings, beverage mixers, non-dairy creamers, coatings, flavorings, powdered and frozen desserts, ice cream and custards, toppings, donut preparations, pickles, relishes, and powdered yeasts.

Sorbitan fatty-acid esters, like all fatty-acid products, are produced from both animal and vegetable sources. Kashruth may be guaranteed only when manufacture is

under full and effective kashruth control of all raw materials and the entire production process.
(See also TALLOW.)

SORBITOL

Sorbitol is produced from corn sugars, glucose, and dextrose. Sorbitol is used as both a sweetener and humectant, maintaining moisture and freshness in baked goods, candies, fondants, toppings, shredded coconut, and jellies. In dietetic beverages and foods, it is used to reduce the aftertaste of artificial sweeteners.

Sorbitol is added to processed meats in order to inhibit browning (carmelization) when heated, which occurs when cane or corn sugars are used.

Sorbitol is approximately two-thirds as sweet as sugar, and identical in caloric content; however, it is distinct from other sugars in that it is metabolized by the body without insulin. In addition, sorbitol does not cause tooth decay. Because of its qualities sorbitol is used in many dietetic foods and candies.

SPAN – see SORBITAN FATTY-ACID ESTERS

SULFONATED INDIGO – see FOOD COLORING

STANNOUS CHLORIDE

Stannous chloride is produced from tin. It is used as a preservative in soft drinks and canned foods.

STEARIC ACID

Stearic acid is a fatty acid found in both animal and vegetable fats, and is commercially produced from either.

Stearates produced from stearic acid are used as lubricants, dispersing agents, anti-caking agents in many powdered preparations, in the formation and coating of tablets; and in the manufacture of glycerides and polysorbates.

Since stearic acid, like all fatty-acid products, is produced from both animal and vegetable sources, kashruth may be guaranteed only when manufacture is under full and effective kashruth control of all raw materials and the entire production process.

(See also TALLOW.)

STEAROYL LACTYLATES

As indicated by its name, stearoyl lactylate is produced from stearic acid, of either animal or vegetable origin, which is reacted with lactic acid. It is then neutralized with either calcium or sodium.

Stearoyl lactylate (calcium, sodium) is a highly effective dough conditioner used to improve volume, appearance and texture; and to retard the staling process of baked goods. Stearoyl lactylate is also used as an additive in specialty bakers' shortenings. It is a common ingredient in coffee whiteners, whipped toppings, puddings, sauces, gravies and dehydrated potatoes.

Since stearoyl lactylate, like all fatty-acid products, is produced from both animal and vegetable sources, kashruth may be guaranteed only when manufacture is under full and effective kashruth control of all raw materials and the entire production process.

SULFUR DIOXIDE and SULFITES

Sulfur dioxide and sulfites (sodium sulfite, potassium sulfite, sodium bisulfite, potassium bisulfite, sodium meta bisulfite, potassium meta bisulfite) are produced from sulfur, a mineral derivative.

The use of sulfur dioxide and sulfites is vital in the production of wine, some fruit juices, carbonated beverages, dried fruits and vegetables as an anti-microbial agent and preservative.

Outside of the United States sulfur dioxide and sulfites may also be used in liquid and dried egg products, fresh meats, meat products and fish. In the United States their use in these foods is prohibited.

SYNTHETIC

The term "synthetic" often confuses consumers who do

not know whether or not to assume a product is kosher simply because it is synthetically produced.

The description "synthetic" indicates that a substance is formed by use of materials and processes other than those of the natural product, and that the end product is a duplicate of the natural substance.

A synthetic chemical process may involve the use of chemicals or other materials of non-kosher as well as kosher origin. Unless the source of all materials and their derivation is established, the fact that it is described as synthetic, or of chemical origin, is not an effective kashruth guarantee.

TALLOW

Tallow — the fat of sheep and cattle — is a primary source for fatty acids, stearic and oleic.

Tallow may also be processed and produced into a shortening, either by itself or in combination with vegetable or animal fats.

The term "tallow" rarely, if ever, appears on product ingredient lists, however, its derivatives are used to produce a variety of food and flavor chemical additives, and the kashruth professional must be aware of their nature. (See also FLAVORS; GLYCERIDES; STEARIC ACID.)

TAPIOCA

Tapioca is a starch derived from the roots of the cassava plant.

It is used as a thickener in soups, dressings and popular pudding preparations.

TARTARIC ACID — see CREAM OF TARTAR

TBHQ

TBHQ (tertiary butyl hydro quinone) is a petrochemical derivative.

It is most commonly used in combination with BHA and BHT as an anti-oxidant for fats and oils.

THIAMIN (VITAMIN B^{1})

Thiamin is a nutrient found in whole grains, rice, meats, eggs, milk, and green-leaf vegetables. Thiamin is produced by chemical synthesis for commercial use.
(See also VITAMINS.)

THIOLS — see FLAVORS

TRIPHENYL-METHANE DYES — see FOOD COLORING

TURMERIC

Turmeric is a spice produced from an herb found in East India and commercially available as a ground powder or oleoresin extract. In the oleoresin form, glycerides and vegetable oils are added to dilute the turmeric and make it soluble in water.

Turmeric is most commonly used in pickles, where it not only adds flavor, but color, as well. It is also used in condiments, soup bases, processed meats and other food preparations where its yellowish-green color and flavor characteristics are desired.

Since oleoresin turmeric is produced with glycerides and vegetable oil, the kosher origin of the diluting materials must be effectively kashruth controlled in order to guarantee kashruth.
(See also OLEORESINS.)

TWEEN — see POLYSORBATES

VANILLA

Vanilla is extracted from the bean of the vanilla plant by percolating the beans in alcohol.

Vanilla is used as a flavoring in many foods, including beverages, baked goods, candies, syrups, puddings and ice cream.

In addition to alcohol, vanilla extract may be formulated in a base to which either water, propylene glycol, sugar, corn syrup or glycerine has been added. Kashruth control is necessary to guarantee the kosher origin of the extract formulation.

VANILLIN

Vanillin is a natural component of vanilla, commercially produced from lignin, the waste material of wood pulp.

It is used as a flavoring agent similar to vanilla.

VEGETABLE OIL — see HYDROGENATED VEGETABLE SHORTENING

VELTOL — see MALTOL

VINEGAR — see ACETIC ACID

VITAMINS

The fact that a vitamin source is indicated to be of synthetic origin does not guarantee that the tablet, capsule or liquid formula is kosher. In the preparation of vitamin formulae, tablets are coated with various substances — waxes, resins, gelatin — in which glycerine and glycerides form part of the coating. Capsules are made from gelatin.

Many tablets are prepared with other additives to help in the binding and forming of the tablet. Various starches, dextrose, lactose, stearates and gelatin may be used for this purpose.

Liquid vitamins often contain glycerine which is used as a base for the formula preparation. In each instance, therefore, the status of all components must be verified to guarantee kashruth, in addition to the source of the vitamin itself.

(See also ACEROLA; ASCORBIC ACID; LANOLIN; RIBOFLAVIN; THIAMIN.)

WHEY

Whey is a by-product of cheese production, and is produced from the liquid residue of the milk which is drained off after the solid curds (cheese) are removed.

After processing and spray-drying, whey is an excellent and inexpensive source of dairy protein, and is used as a replacement for dried milk in many commercially prepared foods.

It is used in the production of cheese, lactose, ice cream,

dairy confections, baked goods, beverages, infant formulas, soups, candies and prepared cereals.

Since whey is a by-product of cheese, it may be accepted as kosher only when produced from cheese made with kosher rennet.
(See also RENNET.)

XANTHAN GUM

Xanthan gum was originally developed by the United States Department of Agriculture as part of a program to find new uses for corn products. It is produced by the bacterial fermentation of corn sugars or other carbohydrates.

Xanthan gum is used as a stabilizer, thickener, emulsifier, and foam enhancer. It is used in the preparation of cottage cheese and other dairy products, puddings, relishes, salad dressings, flavorings, beer and other foamy beverages and beverage mixers.

XANTHINE; XANTHOPHYLL — see FOOD COLORING

XYLITOL

Xylitol is derived from wood pulp wastes, peanut shells, cottonseed husks, or corn cobs.

It is used as an artificial sweetener in tooth pastes and dietetic foods.

YEAST

Yeast are one-celled microorganisms (fungi) whose enzymes cause fermentation and convert sugar into alcohol and carbon dioxide.

For commercial use, masses of yeast cells are pressed and mixed with various starches to form cakes, and are sold as packaged yeast.

Cultured strains of yeast are used in the production of baked goods, wine, beer, alcohol, protein flavor enhancers (nucleatides) and food supplements. They are most commonly derived as a by-product of the brewing process of cereal grains.

Strains of yeast especially suited for wine production are cultivated as well, and are invaluable in the production of the various varieties of wine. They are derived from centuries-old strains of wine yeast.

YELLOW PRUSSIATE OF SODA

Yellow prussiate of soda is a mineral or chemical derivative.

It is used as an anti-caking agent in salt, spice preparations and many powdered foods.

ZEIN

Zein is a protein extracted from corn. It is used as a source of protein in food additives, and as a coating for processed foods.
(See also PHENYLALANINE.)

Appendix: Properly Scaled Fishes and Non-kosher Fishes

Introduction*

Keeping up with kosher and non-kosher commercial fishes is becoming a more and more arduous task. International traffic in food fishes and fish products continues to accelerate. Human populations are growing exponentially while the number of fishes is decreasing as a result of the double onslaught of overfishing and habitat destruction. Consequently, fish mongers must go farther and farther afield to find the fish they need to fill their orders. Moreover, the world-wide search for substitute or

* The author is grateful to his long-time friend, Dr. James W. Atz, Ph.D., Curator Emeritus, Department of Herpetology and Ichthyology of the American Museum of Natural History, New York.

Dr. Atz has graciously extended his services to research and compile a world-wide list of properly scaled fish, in order to share his knowledge with the Jewish community.

We are privileged to publish his work, and we are thankful that this volume has been thus enriched.

Y.L.

supplements for the always-limited supplies of culinary favorites like the red snapper or the pompano has never ceased. This means that species new to our markets are appearing with greater frequency than ever before. The question inevitably arises: Are they kosher?

The new "orange roughy" provides a good example of the kind of problems that can arise in this situation. In 1982 a fish entirely new to the United States arrived from New Zealand. It found a ready market, and soon "orange roughy" appeared in supermarkets and restaurants. The question as to whether or not it was kosher was not an easy one to answer, inasmuch as the fish was available only in the form of frozen fillets. A search of our natural history museums failed to reveal a single specimen. Not until 1987, when intact individuals were specially shipped to us by New Zealand ichthyologists, were we able to determine that the "orange roughy" was indeed properly scaled.

All this indicated that a carefully compiled list of properly scaled fishes such as this forms an essential, but not necessarily sufficient, tool to solve problems that may arise. New fishes may be expected to arrive at any time, and even well-known species can present problems when names get changed or new methods of marketing are introduced. Whenever a question arises, the only safe procedure is to consult with a rabbinical authority.

The most troublesome feature of any check-list is the identification of the items that comprise it. From the beginning, the popular names of the 25,000 or so different kinds of fishes have presented problems. What one fisherman calls a trout, another insists is a bass. When a New Zealander speaks of a cod, he has in mind a fish entirely different from the common codfish most people in Europe and North America know so well. The term "perch" has been deliberately applied to at least a dozen widely different and unrelated kinds of fish. Fortunately, in more and more countries, "official" lists are being adopted, and we have consulted these in preparing our own list. Nevertheless, it must be kept in mind tht a single fish may have more than one accepted popular name. (In contrast, its scientific designation is unique.) In order to make users of this list aware of potential sources of confusion, cross-references have been provided.

The most efficient way to search for a particular name is to look for it in the properly scaled fish section; non-kosher groups are cross-referenced there and appear in italics. To minimize the chance of mistaking a non-kosher fish for a kosher one, certain Families have been treated as non-kosher even though they contain species that are properly finned and scaled. These Families include few, if any, commercially important forms, and they generally not well known except to ichthyologists interested in fish classification. In these cases, the dangers of misidentification outweigh the possible benefits of enjoying a few more acceptable food fishes. (These groups are: Blennies, Cusk-eels, Eel-pouts, Gobies, Gunnels, Pricklebacks, Remoras, Stargazers, Surgeonfishes, and Toadfishes.)

A word of caution ought to be given regarding the new fabricated seafood products such as fish meal. Inasmuch as these are concocted of untold numbers of fishes, caught by the ton and turned into a mass-produced product, no one could ever guarantee that no non-kosher individual fish had slipped into a particular batch. Although some fishes are prepared to look and taste like shellfish, the reverse process does not seem to have been attempted. Similarly, the non-kosher whale and dolphin or porpoise (mammals) meat has never been confused with that of the properly scaled dolphin fish.

James W. Atz, Ph.D.

Curator Emeritus
Department of Herpetology and Ichthyology
American Museum of Natural History

Properly Scaled Fish

Aholehole See: Flagfishes
Albacore See: Mackerels
Alewife See: Herrings
Alfonsin See: Roughies
Alligatorfishes *(non-kosher)*
Amberjack See: Jacks
Anchovies (Family Engraulidae)
European anchovy (Engraulis encrasicolus)
California anchovy (Engraulis mordax)
Cape anchovy (Engraulis japonicus)
Anchoveta (Cetengraulis mysticetus)
Angelfishes (Family Pomacanthidae)
Angelfishes (Holacanthus species, Pomacanthus species)
Argentines or herring-smelts (Family Argentinidae)
Silverside or snodgall (Argentina elongata)
Australian salmons (Family Arripidae)
Australian salmon (Arripis trutta)
Tommy rough (Arripis georgionus)
Ayu (Plecoglossus altivelis)
Ballyhoo See: Flyingfishes
Barb See: Carps
Barracouta See: Snake-mackerels
Barracudas (Family Sphyraenidae)
Barracudas and kakus (Sphyraena species)
Bass See: Drums; Freshwater basses; Sea basses; Sunfishes; Temperate basses
Batfish See: Spadefishes and batfishes
Beluga *See: Sturgeons (non-kosher)*
Beryx (Beryx decadactylus)
Bigeyes (Family Priacanthidae)
Bigeyes or aweoweos (Priacanthus species)
Blackcod See: Sablefishes
Blackfish See: Carps; Wrasses
Blacksmith See: Damselfishes
Blenny *(non-kosher)*
Blueback See: Flounders; Herrings; Trouts
Bluefish, snapper blue, elf or **tailor** (Pomatomus saltatrix)
Bluegill See: Sunfishes
Bocaccio See: Scorpionfishes

Bonefish (Albula vulpes)

Bonito See: Cobia; Mackerels

Bowfin, freshwater dogfish or **grindle** (Amia calva)

Bream See: Butterfly-breams; Carps; Grunters; Pomfrets; Porgies

Brill See: Flounders

***Brotulas** See: Cusk-eels (non-kosher)*

Buffalofish See: Suckers

***Bullhead** See: Catfishes (non-kosher)*

Burbot See: Codfishes

Butterfishes (Family Stromateidae)
Butterfishes and harvestfish (Peprilus species)
Pacific pompano (Peprilus simillimus)
See also: Scats

Butterfly-breams or **threadfin breams** (Family Nemipteridae)
Butterfly-breams (Nemipterus species, Pentapodus species)
Spinecheeks (Scolopis species)

Butterflyfishes (Family Chaetodontidae)
Butterflyfishes (Chaetodon species, Chelmon species)
Longnose butterflyfishes (Forcipiger species)

***Cabezon** See: Sculpins (non-Kosher)*

Calico bass See: Sunfishes

Capelin See: Smelts

Carps and minnows (Family Cyprinidae)
Common carp, mirror carp, leather carp (Cyprinus carpio)
Crucian carp (Carassius carassius)
Goldfish (Carassius auratus)
Minnows (Phoxinus species, Notropis species, etc.)
Breams (Abramis species, Blicca species)
Barbs or barbels (Barbus species, Puntuis species)
Ide (Leuciscus idus)
Daces (Leuciscus leuciscus, Rhinichthys species)
Roach (Rutilus rutilus)
Rudd (Scardinius erythrophthalmus)
Tench (Tinca tinca)
Gudgeon (Gogio gobio)
Shiners (Notropis species)
Chubs (Gila species, Hybopsis species, Nocomis species, Semotilus species)
Splittails (Pogonichthys species)
Squawfishes (Ptychocheilus species)
Sacramento blackfish or hardhead (Orthodon microlepidotus)
Grasscarp (Ctenopharyngodon idella)
Bighead carp (Aristichthys nobilis)
Silver carp (Hypophthalmichthys molitrix)
Indian major carps (Catla catla, Labeo species, Cirrhinus species)

Carpsucker See: Suckers

Caviar See: Trouts and whitefishes (salmon); *Sturgeons (non-kosher); Lumpsuckers (non-Kosher)*

Cero See: Mackerels

Channel bass See: Drums

Char See: Trouts

Chilipepper See: Scorpionfishes

Chinook salmon See: Trouts

Chub See: Carps; Sea chubs; Trouts

Cichlids (Family Cichlidae)
Tilapias (Tilapia species, Oreochromis species, Sarotherodon species)
Cichlids (Cichlasoma species, Haplochromis species, etc.)
Chromides (Etroplus species)

Cigarfish See: Jacks

Cisco See: Trouts

Coalfish See: Codfishes

Cobia, cabio or **black bonito** (Rachycentron canandum)

Cod See: Codfishes; Deepsea cods; Greenlings; Sablefishes; Scorpionfishes; Sea basses; Sleepers; Temperate basses

Codfishes (Family Gadidae)
Cod (Gadus morhua)
Haddock (Melanogrammus aeglefinus)
Pacific cod (Gadus macrodephalus)
Pollock, saithe, or coalfish (Pollachius virens)
Walleye pollock (Theragra chalcogramma)
Arctic cod (Boreogadus saida)
Hakes (Urophycis species)
Whiting (Merlangius merlangus)
Blue whiting or poutassou (Micromesistius poutassou)
Ling (Molva species)
Tomcods or frostfishes (Microgadus species)
Burbot, lawyer, or freshwater ling (Lota lota)
Not including the non-kosher:
Torsk (Brosme brosme)
Five-bearded rockling (Ciliata mustela)

Coho salmon See: Trouts

Corbina or **corvina** See: Drums

Cottonwick See: Grunts

Crappie See: Sunfishes

Crevalle See: Jacks

Curcian carp See: Carps

Cubbyu See: Drums

Cunner See: Wrasses

***Cusk-eels** (non-kosher)*

***Cutlassfishes** (non-kosher)*
Dab See: Flounders
Damselfishes (Family Pomacentridae)
Garibaldi (Hypsypops rubicundus)
Blacksmith (Chromis punctipinnis)
Deepsea cods (Family Moridae)
Blue hake (Antimora rostrata)
Pacific flatnose (Antimora microlepis)
Moro (Mora moro)
Red cod (Physiculus bachus)
Bearded cod (Physiculus barbatus)
Doctorfish See: Surgeonfishes
Dogfish See: Bowfin; *Sharks (non-kosher)*
Dolly varden See: Trouts
Dolphin fishes or **mahimahis** (Coryphaena species)
[Not to be confused with the non-kosher mammal, the dolphin.]
***Dragonets** (non-kosher)*
Drums, croakers or **kobs** (Family Sciaenidae)
Seatrouts and corvinas (Cynoscion species)
Weakfish (Cynoscion nebulosus)
White seabass (Cynoscion nobilis)
Croakers (Micropogonias species, Bairdiella species, Odontoscion species)
Silver perch (Bairdiella chrysoura)
White or king croaker (Genyonemus lineatus)
Black croaker (Cheilotrema saturnum)
Spotfin croaker (Roncador stearnsi)
Yellowfin croaker (Umbrina roncador)
Drums (Pogonias species, Stellifer species, Umbrina species)
Red drum or channel bass (Sciaenops ocellatus)
Freshwater drum (Aplodinotus grunniens)
Kingfishes or king whitings (Menticirrhus species)
California corbina (Menticirrhus undulatus)
Spot or lafayette (Leiostomus xanthurus)
Queenfish (Seriphus politus)
Cubbyu or ribbonfish (Equetus umbrosus)
Jewfish (Argyrosomus hololepidotus)
Drummer See: Sea chubs
***Eelpout** (non-Kosher)*
***Eel** See: Eels; Eelpouts; Cusk-eels; Lampreys (all non-kosher)*
Emperors (Family Lethrinidae)
Emperors (Lethrinus species)
Sweetlips (Lethrinus species)
Eulachon See: Smelts
Flagtails (Family Kuhliidae)
Aholehole (Kuhlia sandvicensis)

Flagtails (Kuhlia species)
Pygmy perches (Edelia species, Nannoperca species)

Flatheads (Platycephalus species, Cociella species, Suggrundus species, etc.)

Flounders (Families Bothidae and Pleuronectidae)
Flounders (Paralichthys species, Liopsetta species, Platichthys species, etc.)
Starry flounder (Platichyths stellatus)
Summer flounder or fluke (Paralichthys dentatus)
Yellowtail flounder (Limanda ferrugina)
Winter flounder, lemon sole, or blackback (Pseudopleuronectes americanus)
Halibuts (Hippoglossus species)
California halibut (Paralichthys californicus)
Bigmouth sole (Hippglossina stomata)
Butter or scalyfin sole (Iopsetta isolepis)
"Dover" sole (Microstomus pacificus)
"English" sole (Parophrys vetulus)
Fantail sole (Xystereurys liolepis)
Petrale sole (Eopsetta jordani)
Rex sole (Glyptocephalus zachirus)
Rock sole (Lepidopsetta bilineata)
Sand sole (Psettichthys melanostictus)
Slender sole (Lyopsetta exilis)
Yellowfin sole (Limanda aspera)
Pacific turbots (Pleuronichthys species)
Curlfin turbot or sole (Pleuronichthys decurrens)
Diamond turbot (Hypsopsetta guttulata)
Greenland turbot or halibut (Rheinhardtius hippoglossoides)
Sanddabs (Citharichthys species)
Dabs (Limanda species)
American plaice (Hippoglossoides platessoides)
European plaice (Pleuronectes platessa)
Brill (Scophthalmus rhombus)
Not including the non-kosher:
European turbot (Scophthalmus maximus)

Fluke See: Flounders

Flying fishes and **halfbeaks** or **garfishes** (Family Exocoetidae)
Flying fishes (Cypselurus species, etc.)
Ballyhoo or balao (Hemiramphus species)
Garfishes (Arrhamphus sclerolepis, Hemiramphus species)

Freshwater basses See: Temperate basses; Sunfishes

Frostfish See: Codfishes; *Cutlassfishes (non-kosher)*

Fugu *See: Puffers (non-kosher)*

Gag See: Sea basses

Galaxias *(non-kosher)*

Gar See: Needle fishes; Flying fishes; *Gars (non-kosher)*

Garibaldi See: Damselfishes
Giant kelpfish (Heterostichus rostratus)
Gizzard shad See: Herrings
Gnomefish (Scombrops boops)
Goatfishes or **surmullets** (Family Mullidae)
Goatfishes (Mullus species, Pseudupeneus species)
Wekes (Mulloidichthys species, Upeneus species)
Kumu (Parupeneus porphyreus)
Red mullet (Mullus surmuletus)

Goby (non-kosher)
Goldeye and **mooneye** (Hiodon alosoides and Hiodon tergisus)
Goldfish See: Carps
Gouramies (Suborder Anabantoidei)
Gouramies (Trichogaster species)
Giant gourami (Osphronemus goramy)
Kissing gourami (Helostoma temmincki)
Climbing perches (Anabas species, Ctenopoma species)

Grasscarp See: Carps
***Grayfish** See: Sharks (non-kosher)*
Grayling See: Trouts
Graysby See: Sea basses
Greenbone (Odax pullus)
Greenlings (Family Hexagrammidae)
Greenlings (Hexagrammos species)
Kelp greenling or seatrout (Hexagrammos decagrammus)
Lingcod, cultus, or blue cod (Ophiodon elongatus)
Atka mackerel (Pleurogrammus monopterygius)

Grenadiers or **rattails** (Family Macrouridae)
Grindle See: Bowfin
Groper See: Sea basses; Temperate basses
Grouper See: Sea basses
Grunion See: Silversides
Grunters or **thornfishes** (Family Teraponidae)
Grunters or thornfishes (Terapon species, Hephaestus species, Scortum species, etc.)
Perches (Leiopotherapon species, Bidyanus species, Amniabata species)
Black breams (Hephaestus fulginosus, Bidyanus welchi)

Grunts (Family Pomadasyidae)
Grunts (Haemulon species, Pomadasys species)
Margate (Haemulon album)
Tomtate (Haemulon aurolineatum)
Cottonwick (Haemulon melanurum)
Sailors choice (Haemulon parrai)
Porkfish (Anisotremus virginicus)

Black margate (Anisotremus surinamensis)
Sargo (Anisotremus davidsoni)
Pigfish (Orthopristis chrysoptera)
Sweetlips and rubberlips (Plectorhynchus species, etc.)

Gunnel (non-kosher)

Gurnard See: Searobins; *Armored gurnards (non-kosher); Flying gurnards (non-kosher)*

Haddock See: Codfishes

Hakes (Family Merlucciidae)
Hakes (Merluccius species)
Silver hake or whiting (Merluccuis bilinearis)
Pacific hake or merluccio (Merluccius productus)
See also: Codfishes; Deepsea cods; Hakes

Halfbeak See: Ballyhoo; Garfishes

Halfmoon See: Sea chubs

Halibut See: Founders

Hamlet See: Sea basses

Hardhead See: Carps

Hardyhead See: Silversides

Harvestfish See: Butterfishes

Hawkfishes (Cirrhitus species)

Herrings (Family Clupeidae)
Atlantic and Pacific herring (Clupea harengus)
Thread herrings (Opisthonemus species)
Shads (Alosa species)
Shad, glut herring, or blueback (Alosa aestivalis)
Hickory shad (Alosa pseudoharengus)
Gizzard shads (Dorosoma species)
Menhadens or mossbunkers (Brevoortia species)
Spanish sardine (Sardinella aurita)
European sardine or pilchard (Sardina pilchardus)
Pacific sardine and pilchards (Sardinops species)
Sprat (Sprattus sprattus)

Hind See: Sea basses

Hogchoker See: Soles

Hogfish See: Wrasses

Horse mackerel See: Jacks

***Icefish** or **noodlefish** (non-kosher)*

Icefishes (Family Nototheniidae)
Cod-icefishes (Notothenia species, Trematomus species, Dissostichus species, Pleurogramma species, etc.)
Not including other Anarctic fishes

Jack mackerel See Jacks

Jacks and **pompanos** (Family Carangidae)
Pompanos, palometas, permits (Trachinotus species)
Amberjacks and yellowtails (Seriola species)

California yellowtail (Seriola dorsalis)
Japanese yellowtail (Seriola quinqueradiata)
Scads, cigarfish, massbanker (Decapterus species, Selar species, Trachurus species)
Jack mackerel or horse mackerel (Trachurus species)
Jacks, kingfishes, uluas (Caranx species, Carangoides species)
Crevalles (Caranx species)
Blue runner (Caranx crysos)
Rainbow runner (Elagatis bipinnulata)
Moonfishes (Vomer species)
Lookdown (Selene vomer)
Black pomfret (Parastromateus niger)
Not including the non-kosher:
Leatherjacket (Oligoplites saurus)
Leatherback or lae (Scomberoides sanctipetri)
Queenfishes (Scomberiodes species)

Jacksmelt See: Silversides
Jewfish See: Sea basses; Drums; *Catfishes (non-kosher)*
John dory (Zeus faber)
Kelpfish See: Giant kelpfish; Greenbone; Kelp-salmon
Kingfish See: Drums; Jacks; Mackerels
Kingklip *See: Cusk-eels (non-kosher)*
Kob See: Drums
Ladyfish or **tenpounder** (Elops saurus)
Lake herring See: Trouts
Lamprey *(non-kosher)*
Lanternfishes (Family Myctophidae)
Largemouth bass See: Sunfishes
Launce or **lance** See: Sand lances
Lawyer See: Codfishes
Leatherback *and* ***leatherjacket*** *See: Jacks (non-kosher)*
Ling See: Codfishes; *Cusk-eels (non-kosher)*
Lingcod See: Greenlings
Lizardfishes (Family Synodontidae)
Lookdown See: Jacks
Mackerels and tunas (Family Scombridae)
Mackerels (Scomber species, Scomberomorus species, Auxis species)
Spanish mackerel, cero, sierra (Scomberomorus species)
King mackerel or kingfish (Scomberomorus cavalla)
Bonitos (Sarda species)
Wahoo (Acanthocybium solanderi)
Tunas (Thunnus species, Euthynnus species)
Skipjack tunas (Euthynnus species, Katsuwonus species)
Albacore (Thunnus alalunga)
See also: Greenlings; Jacks; Snake-mackerels

Mahimahi See: Dolphin fishes

Margate See: Grunts

***Marlin** See: Billfishes (non-kosher)*

Menhaden See: Herrings

Menpachil See: Squirrelfishes

Merluccio See: Hakes

***Midshipman** See: Toadfishes (non-kosher)*

Milkfish or **awa** (Chanos chanos)

Minnow See: Carps; *Galaxias (non-kosher)*

Mojarras (Family Gerreidae)
  Mojaras and pursemouths (Eucinostomus species, Gerres species, Diapterus species)

***Mola** (non-kosher)*

***Monkfish** See: Angel sharks (non-kosher); Goosefishes (non-kosher)*

Mooneye See: Goldeye

Moonfish See: Jacks

Morwongs (Family Cheilodactylidae)
  Morwongs (Cheilodactylus species, Nemadactylus species, etc.)
  Tarakihi (nemadactylus macropterus)

Mossbunker See: Herrings

Mouthbrooder See: Cichlids

Mullets (Family Mugilidae)
  Mullets and amaamas (Mugil species, Liza species)
  Striped or gray mullet or bully (Mugil cephalus)
  Uouoa (Neomyxus chaptalii)
  Mountain mullets or dajaos (Agonostomus species)
See also: Goatfishes

Murrel See: Snakehead

Muskellunge See: Pikes

Mutton hamlet See: Sea basses

Muttonfish See: Snappers

Needlefishes or **marine gars** (Family Belonidae)
  Needlefishes (Strongylura species, Tylosurus species, etc.)
  Houndfish (Tylosurus crocodilus)

***Oilfish** (non-kosher)*

Opaleye See: Sea chubs

Orange roughy See: Roughies

***Paddlefish** See: Sturgeons (non-kosher)*

Palometa See: Jacks

Parrotfishes (Family Scaridae)
  Parrotfishes and uhus (Scarus species, Sparisoma species, etc.)

Perches (Family Percidae)
Yellow perch (Perca flavescens)
European perch (Perca fluviatilis)
Walleye, pikeperch, or yellow walleye (Stizostedion vitreum)
Sauger (Stizostedion)
Zander or pikeperch (Stizostedion lucioperca)
Ruffe (Gymnocephalus cernua)
Darters (Percina species, Etheostoma species, Ammocrypta species)
See also: Drums; Flagtails; Gouramies; Grunters; Sandperches; Scorpionfishes; Sea basses; Snappers; Surfperches; Temperate basses

Permit See: Jacks

Picarels (Centracanthus species, Spicara species)

Pickerel See: Pikes

Pigfish See: Grunts

Pikes (Family Esociade)
Pike (Esox lucius)
Pickerels (Esox species)
Muskellunge (Esox masquinongy)
See also: Perches

Pilchard See: Herrings

Pinfish See: Porgies

Plaice See: Flounders

Pollock See: Codfishes

Pomfrets (Family Bramidae)
Ray's bream or pomfret (Brama brama)
Pomfrets (Brama species, Pterycombus species)
See also: Jacks

Pompano See: Jacks; Butterfishes

Ponyfishes (Family Leiognathidae)
Soapies (Gazza species, Secutor species)
Slimies (Leiognathus species)

Porgies and **seabream** (Family Sparidae)
Porgies (Calamus species, Diplodus species, Pagrus species, etc.
Scup (Stenotomus chrysops)
Pinfish (Lagodon rhomboides)
Sheepshead (Archosargus probatocephalus)
Carpenter (Argyrozona argyrozona)
Steenbrases (Petrus rupestris, Lithognathus species)
Musselcrackers (Sparodon species)
Stumpnoses (Rhabdosargus species)
Red seabream (Pagrus major)

Porkfish See: Grunts

Pout *See: Eelpouts (non-kosher)*

Poutassou See: Codfishes

Prickleback *(non-kosher)*
Pursemouth See: Mojarras
Queenfish See: Drums; *Jacks and pompanos (non-kosher)*
Quillback See: Suckers
Rabalo See: Snooks
Rabbitfishes or spinefoots (Siganus species)
Ratfish *(non-kosher)*
Rattail See: Grenadiers
Ray *(non-kosher)*
Ray's bream See: Pomfrets
Redfish See: Scorpionfishes; Wrasses
Redhorse See: Suckers
Red snapper See: Snappers
Remora *(non-kosher)*
Roach See: Carps
Rock bass See: Sunfishes
Rockcod See: Sea basses; Scorpionfishes
Rockfish See Scorpionfishes; Temperate basses
Rock hind See: Sea basses
Rosefish See: Scorpionfishes
Roughies or slimeheads (Family Trachichthyidae)
Orange roughy (Hoplostethus atlanticus)
Alfonsin (Hoplostethus mediterraneus)
Sawbellies or roughies (Hoplostethus species)
Not including the non-kosher:
Roughies (Trachichthys species)
Rudderfish See: Sea chubs
Runner See: Jacks
Sablefishes (Family Anoplopomatidae)
Sablefish or black cod (Anoplopoma fimbria)
Skilfish (Erilepis zonifer)
Sailfish *See: Billfishes (non-kosher)*
Sailors choice See: Grunts
Saithe See: Codfishes
Salmon See: Trouts; Australian salmons; Sea basses
Sandeel, beaked sandfish, or **beak-salmon** (Gonorynchus gonorynchus)
Sandfish *(non-kosher)*
Sand lances, sand launces or **sand eels** (Ammodytes species)
Sandperches or **sandsmelts** (Family Parapercidae)
Bluecod (Parapercis colias)
Sandsmelts (Parapercis species)
Sardine See: Herrings

Sargo See: Grunts

Sauger See: Perches

Sauries (Family Scomberesocidae)

Saury (Scomberesox saurus)
Pacific saury (Cololabis saira)

Scad See: Jacks

Scats or **butterfishes** (Family Scatophagidae)

Scats or butterfishes (Scatophagus species)
Butterfish (Selenotoca multifasciata)

Scamp See: Sea basses

Schoolmaster See: Snappers

Scorpionfishes (Family Scorpaenidae)

Scorpionfishes (Scorpaena species)
California scorpionfish or sculpin (Scorpaena guttata)
Nohus (Scorpaenopsis species)
Redfish, rosefish, or ocean perch (Sebastes marinus)
Rockfishs and rockcods (Sebastes species, Sebastodes species, etc.)
Pacific ocean perch (Sebastes alutus)
Chilipepper (Sebastes goodei)
Bocaccio (Sebastes paucispinis)
Cowcod (Sebastes levis)
Thornyheads (Sebastolobus species)

Scup See: Porgies

Sea basses (Family Serranidae)

Basses (Serranus species, Anthias species, Dicentrarchus labrax)
Groupers (Epinephelus species, Mycteroperca species)
Gropers (Epinephelus species)
Rockcods (Epinephelus species, Cephalopholis species, etc.)
Estuary cod, black-tipped cod, coral cod, etc. (Epinephelus species)
Rock hind (Epinephelus adscensionin)
Speckled hind (Epinephelus drummondahayi)
Red hind (Epinephelus guttatus)
Spotted cabrilla (Epinephelus analogus)
Jewfish (Epinephelus itajara)
Graysby (Epinephelus cruentatus)
Gag (Mycteroperca microlepis)
Scamp (Mycteroperca ohenax)
Hamlets (Hypoplectrus species, Epinephelus afer)
Sand basses and kelp bass (Paralabrax species)
Sand perches (Diplectrum species)
Black sea basses (Centropristis species)
Sea perches (Caesioperca species, Hypoplectrodes species, etc.)
Coral trouts, tiger trout, bar-checked trout, etc. (Plectropoma species)
See also: Drums; Temperate basses

Seabream See: Porgies

Sea-carps (Family Aplodactylidae, Dactylosargus species)

Sea chubs (Family Kyphosidae)
Chubs and drummers (Kyphosus species)
Bermuda chub or rudderfish (Kyphosis sectatrix)
Blackfishes (Girella species)
Opaleye (Girella nigricans)
Halfmoon (Medialuna californiensis)

Seaperch See: Sea basses; Surfperches

Searaven *See: Sculpins (non-kosher)*

Searobins (Family Triglidae)
Searobins (Prionotus species)
Gurnards (Trigla species, Chelodonichthys species)
Not including the non-kosher:
Armored gurnards and flying gurnards

Sea-squab *See: Puffers (non-kosher)*

Seatrout See: Drums; Greenlings; Sea basses; Trout

Shad See: Herrings

Sheephead and **sheepshead** See: Porgies; Wrasses

Sierra See: Mackerels

Sillagos or **smelt-whitings** (Family Sillaginidae)
Sillagos (Sillago species)
Japanese whiting (Sillago japonica)
Spotted whiting (Silloginodes punctatus)

Silversides (Family Atherinidae)
Whitebait, spearing, or silversides (Menidia species)
California grunion (Leuresthes tenuis)
Jacksmelt (Atherinopsis californiensis)
Topsmelt (Atherinops affinis)
Hardyheads (Ceratocephalus species, etc.)
See also: Argentines

Skate *(non-kosher)*

Skipjack See: Mackerels

Sleepers (Family Eleotridae)
Bigmouth sleeper or guavina (Gobiomorus dormitor)
Sleepy cod (Oxyeleotris lineatus)

Smallmouth bass See: Sunfishes

Smelts (Family Osmeridae)
Smelts (Osmerus species, Spirinchus species)
Capelin (Mallotus vilosus)
Eulachon (Thaleichthys pacificus)
Surf smelt (Hypomesus pretiosus)

Snakeheads (Channa species, Ophicephalus species)

Snake mackerels (Family Gempylidae)
Snake mackerel (Gempylus serpens)

Snoek or barracouta (Thyrsites atun)
Escolar (Lepidocybium flavobrunneum)
Not including the non-kosher:
Oilfish (Ruvettus pretiosus)

Snapper blue See: Bluefish

Snappers (Family Lutjanidae)
Snappers (Lutjanus species)
Schoolmaster (Lutjanus apodus)
Red snapper (Lutjanus campechanus)
Muttonfish or mutton snapper (Lutjanus analis)
Mangrove jack (Lutjanus argentimaculatus)
Red emperor (Lutjanus sebae)
Seaperches (Lutjanus species)
Yellowtail snapper (Ocyurus chrysurus)
Kalikali (Pristipomoides sieboldi)
Opakapaka (Pristipomoides microlepis)
Onaga (Etelis carbunculus)

Snoek See: Snake mackerels

Snooks (Family Centropomidae)
Snooks or rabalos (Centropomus species)
Nile perch (Lates niloticus)
Silver barramundi or giant perch (Lates calcarifer)
Perchlets (Ambassis species)
Glassfishes or glassies (Ambassis species)

Sockeye salmon See: Trouts

Soles (Family Soleidae)
Sole or true sole (Solea solea)
Lined sole (Achirus lineatus)
Hogchoker (Trinectes maculatus)
Moses sole or toxic sole (pardachirus marmoratus)
See also: Flounders

Spadefishes (Family Ephippidae)
Spadefishes (Chaetodipterus species)
Batfishes or sea bats (Platax species)

Spanish mackerel See: Mackerels

Spearing See: Silversides

Splittail See: Carps

Spoonbill cat *See: Strugeons (non-kosher)*

Spot See: Drums

Sprat See: Herrings

Squawfish See: Carps

Squirrelfishes or soldierfishes (Family Holocentridae)
Squirrelfishes (Holocentrus species)
Menpachii and soldiers (Myripristis species)

Stargazers *(non-kosher)*

Steelhead See: Trouts

Striped bass See: Temperate basses

***Suckerfishes** See: Remoras (non-kosher)*

Suckers (Family Catostomidae)

Suckers (Catostomus species, Moxostoma species)
Buffalo fishes (Ictiobus species)
Redhorses (Moxostoma species)
Quillback and carpsuckers (Carpiodes species)

Sunfishes (Family Centrarchidae)

Freshwater basses (Micropterus species)
Largemouth bass (Micropterus salmoides)
Smallmouth bass (Micropterus dolomieui)
Sunfishes (Lepomis species)
Bluegill (Lepomis macrochirus)
Warmouth (Lepomis gulosus)
Rock bass or red eye (Ambloplites rupestris)
Crappies or calico basses (Pomois species)
Sacramento perch (Archoplites interruptus)
See also: *Molas (non-kosher)*

Surfperches (Family Embiotocidae)

Surfperches (Amphistichus species, Hyperprosopon species)
Seaperches (Embiotoca species, Hypsurus species, Phanerodon species, Rhacochilus species)
Black perch (Embiotoca jacksoni)
Pile perch (Rhacochilus vacca)
Shiner perch (Cymatogaster aggregata)

Sweetlips See: Emperors; Grunts

***Surgeonfishes** (non-kosher)*

***Tang** See: Surgeonfishes (non-kosher)*

Tarpon (Megalops atlanticus)

Tautog See: Wrasses

Temperate basses (Family Percichthyidae)

Striped bass or rockfish (Morone saxatilis)
Yellow bass (Morone mississippiebsis)
White bass (Morone chrysops)
White perch (Morone americana)
Giant California sea bass (Stereolepis gigas)
Wreckfish (Polyprion americanus)
Estuarine and mountain perches (Macquaria species)
Yellowbelly or golden perch (Macquaria ambigua)
Murray river cods (Maccullochella species)
Troutcod or bluenose (Maccullochella macquariensis)
Gropers (Polyprion species)

Tench See: Carps

Tenpounders See: Ladyfish

Thornfish See: Grunters

Threadfin bream See: Butterfly-breams

Threadfins (Family Polynemidae)
Blue bobo (Polydactylus approximans)
Barbu (Polydactylus virginicus)
Moi (Polydactylus sexfilis)

Tilapia See: Cichlids

Tilefishes (Family Malacanthidae)
Tilefishes (Malacanthus species, Branchiostegus species)
Atlantic tilefish (Lopholatilus chamaeleonticeps)
Ocean whitefish (Caulolatilus princeps)

***Toadfish** (non-kosher)*

Tomcod See: Codfishes

Tomtate See: Grunts

Tonguefishes (Cynoglossus species, Paraplagusia species)

Topsmelt See: Silversides

Tripletail (Lobotes surinamensis)

Trouts and whitefishes (Family Salmonidae)
Atlantic salmon (Salmo salar)
Pacific slamons: sockeye, blueback, or red; chinook, king, or spring; pink or humpback; coho or silver; chum, dog, or fall (Oncorhynchus species)
Trouts; brown; rainbow or steelhead; cutthroat; golden; bull; Apache (Salmo species)
Chars: lake trout; brook trout; arctic char; Dolly Varden (Salvelinus species)
Whitefishes and ciscos (Coregonus species, Prosopium species)
Cisco or lake herring (Coregonus artedii)
Chubs (Coregonus species)
Graylings (Thymallus species)
Not including the non-kosher:
Maori trouts and Mountain trouts (Galaxias species)
See also: Drums; *Galaxies (non-kosher);* Greenlings; Sea basses

Tuna See: Mackerels

***Turbot** See: Flounders (one species non-kosher)*

Wahoo See: Mackerels

Walleye See: Perches

Walleye pollock See: Codfishes

Weakfish See: Drums

White amur See: Grasscarp

Whitebait See: *Galaxies (non-kosher)*; Silversides

Whitefish See: Tilefishes; Trouts

Whiting See: Codfishes; Drums; Hakes; Sillagos

Wrasses (Family Labridae)
Hogfishes and aawas (Bodianus species)
Hogfish or capitaine (Lachnolaimus maximus)

Tautog or blackfish (Tautoga onitis)
Cunner (Tautogolabrus adspersus)
California sheephead or redfish (Semicossyphus pulcher)
Senorita (Oxyjulis californica)

Wreckfish See: Temperate basses

Yellowtail See: Jacks; Mackerels

Non-kosher Fish

Alligatorfishes (Family Agonidae)

Angel sharks or monkfishes (Family Squatinidae)

Armored gurnards (Family Peristediidae)

Billfishes (Family Istiophoridae)
Sailfishes (Istiophorus species)
Marlins and spearfishes (Tetrapterus species, Makaira species)

Blennies (Suborder Blennioidei)
Pikeblennies, klipfishes, kelpfishes, fringeheads, and rockskippers

Catfishes (Order Siluriformes)
Channel catfish (Ictalurus punctatus)
Bullheads (Ictalurus species)
Sea catfishes (Arius species, etc.)
"Walking" catfishes (Clarias species)
Butter jew (Neosilurus ater)

Clingfishes (Family Gobiesocidae)
Rocksucker (Chorisochismus dentex)
Frogfish or pejesapo (Sicyases sanguineus)

Cusk-eels (Family Ophidiidae)
Cusk-eels (Ophidion species, Lepophidium species, etc.)
Lings (Genypterus species)
Kingklip (Genypterus capensis)

Cutlassfishes (Family Trichiuridae)
Cutlassfishes (Trichiurus species)
Cutlassfish or hairtail (Trichiurus lepturus)
Scabbardfishes or frostfishes (Lepidopus species, Benthodesmus species)
Buttersnoek (Lepidopus caudatus)

Dragonets (Family Callionymidae)

Eelpouts (Family Zoarcidae)
Eelpouts (Lycodes species, etc.)
Ocean pout (Macrozoarces americanus)
Viviparous blenny (Zoarces viviparus)

Eels (Order Anguilliformes)
American, European, Japanesse, and Australian eels (Anguilla species)
Conger eel (Conger oceanicus)
Morays (Muraena species, Gymnothorax species, etc.)

Flying gurnards (Family Dactylopteridae)

Galaxias (Family Galaxiidae)
- Whitebait (Galaxias species, Lovetta sealii)
- Maori trouts and mountain trouts (Galaxias species)
- Jollytail, inanga, cowfish, or minnow (Galaxias maculatus)
- Kokopus (Galaxias species)

Gars (Order Semionotiformes)
- Gars (Lepisosteus species)
- Alligator gars (Atractosteus species)

Gobies (Family Gobiidae)

Goosefishes or **anglers** (Lophius species)

Gunnels (Family Pholididae)

Icefishes or **noodlefishes** (Family Salangidae)

Lampreys (Order Petromyzontiformes)

Leatherback and leatherjacket. See: Jacks

Lumpsuckers (Family Cyclopteridae)
- Lumpfish (Cyclopterus lumpus)
- Snailfishes (Liparis species, Careproctus species, etc.)

Molas (Family Molidae)
- Molas (Mola lanceolata and Ranzania laevis)
- Ocean sunfish (Mola mola)

Oilfish (Ruvettus pretiosus)

Pricklebacks (Family Stichaeidae)
- Pricklebacks, cockscombs, warbonnets, shannys (Lumpenus species, Chirolepis species, Anoplarchus species, etc.)

Porcupinefishes (Family Diodontidae)
- Porcupine fish (Diodon hystrix)
- Burrfishes (Chilomycterus species)

Puffers or **blowfishes** (Family Tetraodontidae)
- Puffers, blowfishers, or swellfishes (Sphoeroides species, Lagocephalus species, Fugu species, etc.)
- Sea-squab (Sphoeroides species)
- Tobies or sharpnosed puffers (Canthigaster species)

Ratfish or **chimaeras** (Order Chimaeriformes)
- Ratfishes (Hydrolagus species, Chimaera species)
- Elephantfishes (Callorhinchus species)

Rays (Order Rajiformes)
- Sawfishes (Pristis species)
- Guitarfishes (Rhinobatos species, etc.)
- Electric rays (Torpedo species, etc.)
- Skates (Raja species, etc.)
- Stingrays and butterfly rays (Dasyatis species, etc.)
- Eaglerays (Myliobatis species, etc.)
- Mantas (Manta species, Mobula species)

Remoras (Family Echeneidae)
- Sharksucker (Echeneis naucrates)
- Suckerfisher (Remora species, etc.)

Sandfish (Tricodon trichodon)

Sculpins (Family Cottidae)
- Sculpins (Myoxocephalus species, Cottus species, etc.)
- Cabezon (Scropeanichthys marmoratus)
- Searaven (Hemitripterus americanus)

Sharks (Superorder Selachimorpha)
- Mako shark (Isurus oxyrinchus)
- Grayfishes or dogfishes (Mustelus species, Squalus species)
- Smoothhounds (Mustelus species)
- Soupfin shark (Galeorhinus zyopterus)

Stargazers (Uranoscopidae)
- Stargazers (Uranoscopus species, Astroscopus species, Kathetostoma species)

Sturgeons and **paddlefishes** (Order Acipenseriformes)
- Sturgeons (Acipenser species, Scaphirhynchus species)
- Beluga (Huso huso)
- Paddlefish or spoonbill cat (Polyodon spathula)

Surgeonfishes (Family Acanthuridae)
- Surgeonfishes and tangs (Acanthurus species, Zebrasoma species)
  - Doctorfish (Acanthurus chirugus)
- Unicorn fishes or kalas (Naso species)
- Moorish idols or kihikihis (Zanclus species)

Swordfish (Xiaphias gladius)

Toadfishes (Family Batrachoididae)
- Toadfishes (Opsanus species, etc.)
- Midshipmen (Porichthys species)

Triggerfishes and **filefishes** (Family Balistidae)
- Triggerfishes (Balistes species, Canthidermis species, etc.)
- Filefishes (Cantherhines species, Monacanthus species, etc.)
- Black durgon (Melichthys niger)

Trunkfishes or **boxfishes** (Family Ostraciidae)
- Boxfishes (Ostracion species, Tetrosomus species)
- Trunkfishes and cowfishes (Lactophrys species)

Wolffishes (Family Anarhichadidae)
- Wolffishes or ocean catfishes (Anarhichas species)
- Wolf-eel (Anarrhichthys ocellatus)